A Shit Picker's Guide to Training Horses

A. Pinto Miremadi

This book is dedicated to Christa,
my wife, business partner, and
fellow student of the horse.

WITH THANKS TO

Christa, Phoenix and Zahra Miremadi for their faithful support
and encouragement to write this book, Pat Dymond for reading and
editing it, Daryl Gibb and Miles Kingdon for advice and inspiration in
training horses, and Merly Salzberg and Miles Kingdon
for reading and giving feedback.

Cover photo by Tina Harnett; unless otherwise noted, other photos were
taken by family and friends and used with permission.

CONTENTS

INTRODUCTION

Another horse book? Why? There's so many out there by so many great and amazing equestrian masters let alone a shit picker, what's the point of writing another one?

I was persuaded by my wife and a few other colleagues. As we sat around and talked shop endlessly, they convinced me to pen down my thoughts and lessons learned throughout the years of horsing around. They felt my journey has been unique, somewhat hilarious and would be of value to others.

My perspective was bound to be a little bit different. Primarily a musician with a degree in Philosophy, I was never a horse crazy person and only discovered them by marrying into it almost two decades ago. I didn't grow up with horses and my childhood had nothing to do with ranching except for fanatically watching westerns on T.V.

However, the amount of exposure and time I spent feeding and mucking out after a revolving door of thirty plus horses at a time fast tracked me to an understanding of horses that differed from the average equestrian. I was dealing with various breeds and levels of training, from the newborn Arabians bred on our farm, to retired performers, from mild school horses to wild and problematic training projects with behavioral challenges that ranged from starting to extreme aggression, fear issues and everything in between. The amount of mass exposure and responsibilities that came with being put in charge of managing the herd and maintaining the ranch gave me an understanding that resulted in me becoming a professional horse trainer. Yet, the most valuable lessons I learned about horses were acquired during shit picking.

Although I've consulted and learned from many excellent horsemen/women along the way, as an inexperienced novice with no history in the field, my not-so-coveted starting position as the "shit picker" set the horse as my primary and direct source of knowledge, where I would hear it straight from the horse's mouth, with no preconceived notions or indirect interpretations as to how I should view or understand them.

I had to draw from my own unrelated life experiences to help me survive and pay close attention to the feedback I was getting from the horses. It took me by quite a surprise when I started seeing parallels between music and horsemanship. Timing, feel, rhythm, performance and creativity - I could draw on these experiences as a musician to help me.

Of course maintaining horses requires more than just picking. Many more skills had to be acquired along the way, skills that demanded a basic and practical understanding of mechanics, physics, chemistry, math, geometry, biology, psychology and first aid. You can't build shelters, compost manure, operate machinery, haul trailers, calculate hay consumption and cost, and tend to injured riders and horses without getting a basic handle on these subjects. Horses challenged me to think, to change, to grow, to educate myself, become a problem solver and morph into the kind of person I never imagined I would or could become. They have changed me as a person, just as Rock and Roll has, and they continue to mold me to be who I need to be.

All beings echo different aspects and facets of the universe, but the horse, I think, embodies everything the universe has to offer in one perfect and complete package. Horses have given me the impression that all wisdom and science can be accessed and learned through them if we are willing to pay attention and go the distance. Lessons and secrets that I would discover through mucking up their shit!

Take heed!

This is not a how-to book.

This is a book that documents what I've learned so far through my experiences. I would imagine and hope that I will learn and discover much more, as I'm painfully aware of the fact that I've only begun to scratch the surface of what these majestic animals have to offer.

With that, let the shit show begin!

Pinto and Fire, photo by Tina Harnett

1 COMMUNICATION THROUGH SPATIAL RELATION

I didn't want to be a shit picker. In fact it was my distaste for the job that encouraged me to get more involved with horses, so I could find a better place for myself in the family business. But the more I learned about working with horses the more it became clear to me that it was the mucking and feeding that laid the most valuable foundation for understanding them.

To this day, I insist on picking and feeding my training projects. If I don't, I feel like I may have missed out on some crucial and vital information before stepping into the round pen that could be detrimental to my performance and reading the horse.

If you are paying attention you will realize and capitalize on the golden opportunities available to you during the course of getting simple barn chores done. The most obvious is spending time in each other's space in a "non-training" or "work" setting. This is where the horse is truly at liberty, not just physically but mentally. They are not in work mode and we get to see them as they are, unadulterated by our, most of the time, clumsy training sessions that miss the point or are just not quite right, agenda driven sessions that fail to meet the horse where they're at and fail to establish a meaningful and trusting partnership between you.

A horse moving his shoulders over for you in the round pen is not the same as a horse moving his shoulders for you in the paddock, field or stall when you come in with hay or a pitchfork. The yield of the shoulders in the latter settings are much more meaningful, truthful and reliable than the one you get in the pen even at liberty session.

What do I mean by more reliable? I mean the kind of yield that your horse will give you in the most stressful and inopportune moments as opposed to performing choreographed and practiced routines in a controlled environment. A yield that is given through second nature in times of sheer trouble and emergency, when the stakes are high and the horse's cooperation to your aid is crucial to your and your horse's survival, in times that really count and will keep you alive, not just doing circles in an arena over and over and over again.

If we can see the relevance between ground work and work in saddle, connect the dots as to how our ground work is directly preparing our horse for riding, we can then take one more step back and see how conscious mucking and feeding can in turn set our horses up with an even deeper foundation for partnership that precedes and surpasses the other two stages. What I've described here is a linear progression of connecting the dots when in reality we are talking about something quite three dimensional.

Space.

The space in which you work will play a huge role in setting the "tone" for the conversation and the kind of communication you are trying to achieve with your horse.

The spatial settings not only provide a context that will affect the nature of the interplay but will also determine the type of interaction that would prove more successful given its properties and dimensions.

There is a difference between a horse picking up the canter in the arena as opposed to in open country. The physical boundaries in the arena play a great part in influencing the response you get from your horse. In the open country, you and your horse have to work a lot harder to stay together without the aid and influence of the fences in the arena.

Similarly there's a difference between a horse moving his quarters for you in a stall as opposed to on open acreage.

Asking for space on line, moving quarters

Asking for space, mustang style

Not only have I noticed through my shit picking experiences a significant difference in the way a horse moves during the "non-work" setting as opposed to "work" setting, but I've also noticed yet another level of contrast in movement depending on the size and characteristics of the space we are in: e.g., stall versus paddock versus open field, which will change again depending on the size of the settings.

Is it a 10x10 walled space or larger? Is it 1 acre or a 100? Is it one horse or multiple?

Different spaces promote and accommodate different psychological needs and activities. This idea is commonly used by architects when designing buildings with specific functionalities in mind. The use of space in a hospital as opposed to a private home, spaces designed for social settings as opposed to private, and so on. The space is designed to accommodate a specific type of interaction and, interestingly enough, the space in turn promotes and inspires the intended interactions of its occupants.

A mismatch of the space and intended activity can become problematic, like a bull in a china shop.

Similarly in an equine setting, I would not want to have the kind of conversation I usually have in a round pen with a horse in a tight, crowded tie stall in the barn. The dimensions of the stall and the physical proximity it creates with you and the horse require a much quieter, softer and private "tone" of interaction with your horse. Anything else could result in creating dangerous situations.

Something as basic as the geometrical shape of the space you share with your horse can make all the difference in the world depending on the activity and interaction taking place in it.

A specific incident comes to mind that really drove this point home for me.

Marcelo

I was working with a recently gelded, 16.3 hand warmblood gelding, Marcelo.

Through years of working with horses, I've become a strong believer in preparing your horse to handle whatever it is they're going to encounter in life as a riding horse. So I try to break things down to small achievable steps and move at their pace. Show them something and wait. Give them time. Give them space. Let them think about it. Let them experiment and investigate. Let them test it. For the most part this kind of approach eliminates or significantly reduces the element of surprise, preventing the horse from going into a "running blind" mode where they may end up injuring themselves, something I definitely want to avoid at all cost. I want them to have a positive experience with the whole process, feel confident, ready for the next step before we move on. But, sometimes no matter how much you prepare a horse there's still a chance things might go sideways.

Some horses think they're ready and give you the okay to the next step only to realize they were not quite ready yet. It's not a lie. They just didn't know. Similar to an enthusiastic kid who badly wants to go on the roller coaster. You let them watch. You tell them what will happen and they are psyched and can't wait to get on the ride. They beg you, so you take them. They get in the cart. Still good? Yeah. They get strapped down. Still okay? Uh huh. The coaster starts moving. How do you feel? Great!! The coaster start climbing and they get a little quiet and as you reach the peak just before the fast plummet, they want off! Well. Sorry. Too late.

The best you can do for them at this point is hold their hand, remain calm and try to get them through it. Some will come out feeling like a million bucks and want to go again, some will never want to set foot on a coaster again.

Welcome to the Point of No Return

Working with the horses the way we do, through consent and respect for their comfort level, things can get complicated when it comes to clients. I can never give them a definite answer as to how long it might take to get their horse going. I can only take them as far and as fast as they are willing to go. I work with the horse at their pace and comfort level, and if they don't want to have anything to do with what I'm offering, I'm willing to leave it at that and advise the client to get another trainer. It almost never happens. In fact I can't think of a time that it ever has. But if they want to go slower and slower yet, then that's what we'll do. I have started horses from barely being halter broke to riding the trails in as short a time as three days to as long as two three-month periods stretched out over a whole year.

But no matter how slow or fast you go and how much you prepare them, there's always that one step that has a point of no return. For me, one of those points is the first time you cinch that saddle on. You can't kind of tighten it. If that horse takes off bucking and that saddle is loose and does not stay in place you could end up injuring the horse. There's no in between. You have to cinch it right up. Again, many steps are taken to prepare the horse for the sensation with exit strategies built into them so the horse can have a quick taste and have it go away. I use my lead line around their barrel to mimic the sensation of having a tight cinch; not only that but also getting used to me reaching under their belly, grabbing the end of the rope and tightening it. I can micro manage and control the feeling in short little spurts and release before the horse gets too bothered, gradually working the way up to longer periods with more pressure until the horse is not worried at all about the sensation anymore. Have them carry a saddle around without cinching so they can experience the feel of the weight and the tree, with my hand on the horn so I can pull it off before they get too worried.

This kind of preparation, for the majority of horses, prevents them from ever getting bothered or bucking under saddle, while for others it drastically reduces the intensity of their reaction to it. For the most part they're just testing it instead of running blind. I know this since they register and respond to the support I offer them at the end of the line or at liberty. In contrast, a horse that is running blind will not respond to or register anything, as their flight instinct has overtaken all other faculties.

Once in a while you will come across that one horse who will have a total meltdown during the process and there's really nothing you can do for them but wait for the storm to calm. The cinching is a known point of no return that you can prepare yourself and your horse for with some calculated risks and back-up plans should the worst case scenario occur.

Back to Marcelo

With the warmblood in question, Marcelo, we were at the stage in our training where he had been backed a few times and I had put in a few technical rides on him, meaning he had walked around, turning left, right, stop and back up just a few steps at a time for less than a minute at a time with a bareback pad held on with a cinch. He had felt my legs on his sides and had learned how to yield to the cues coming off them, so when it came time to putting a saddle on him with stirrups I felt he had had plenty of preparation with the sensation of objects rubbing on his sides.

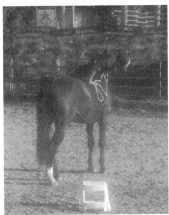 

Marcelo's first backing and ride

Well, as it turned out, I was wrong.

To further break the process down for him and prepare for the next step in our session, I had chosen a treeless western style saddle as opposed to a treed one. It was much closer in feel to the bareback pad with the only difference being stirrups. I had decided to keep him on a 12 foot line, so I could be there for him if he got in trouble and needed support. The saddle went on nice and smooth and he felt the stirrups on his sides with no worries. I worked both sides, picking up the stirrups and letting them back down gently and carefully at first, while becoming progressively more aloof and loud, staying calm, and I rubbed them back and forth to make sure there were no surprises for him once he moved out under the saddle. I wanted him confident in dealing with the stirrups once they started moving more with his increased gait.

So far so good. He seemed relaxed, licking and chewing, blinking, eyes and ears on me, expressing, "Now what?" Well, move out buddy, see how it feels when in motion. He made a full circle at a walk, calm and confident, but at the completion of the first circle and the beginning of a second, the outside stirrup hit the fence panel making a clanking sound that startled him, which made him jump a little, which made the stirrups slam against his barrel on both sides, which made him jump harder, which made the stirrups slam harder, which made him jump worse . . . you get the picture.

The situation escalated lightning fast leaving no time for defusing, disrupting or offering any kind of help or guidance to this upset and troubled horse who was now with each bucking stride working himself up into a complete meltdown and greater volcanic eruptions. Holding on to the rope would have been as futile as trying to hold on to a rocket. He was off and gone with the lead line dangling behind him.

Shit!!!

Not at all how I wanted things to go. But here we were, and it didn't have to be the end of the world. Shit happens. It's happened before, it will happen again. Not to worry, normally after a couple laps, horses gradually calm down to a trot, then a walk and stop, giving me an opportunity to reassure and give them the support they seek after the fact.

Back to the Main Point – Space

Now this is the part of the story that takes us back to the main point, the space in which all this took place.

We were in arena we called the "green arena." It was a deep sand arena rectangular in shape but small in size. About 60'x90'. We called it the green arena because its size limited the amount of speed that could be gained in it, and seemed to slow things down for green horses and green riders to a more comfortable pace. But for the situation I was in, the size was not going to be of any help. That horse was running blind, not at all registering or seeing the fence panels that under better circumstances would regulate and limit his speed. He made the first corner somehow, but not the second. As I watched him head towards the second corner I knew there was no way he was going to make the turn. He was going straight into the fence. It was going to be bad. But "how bad?" I asked myself. "Did I remember to get the client to sign a waiver? How will I tell them their $50k horse flown in from Germany died? Will he die a quick death on his own or will we need to put him down?" And finally and most importantly, "Man! I would give anything to go back in time and change the venue to a round pen instead of this rectangular arena."

I can't always predict or control what the horse is going to do but I can control my own choices and actions. I could have chosen the right venue for this. The round pen. Running blind in the round pen would have avoided the coming disaster I was helplessly watching unfold in front of me as there would have been no corners to contend with. He could have gone on running blind round and round without endangering himself.

But it was too late and I had no time machine.

As predicted he did not make the second turn. He went straight into the metal fence. I exhaled deeply and accepted his and my fate.

A spine-shaking fleshy thud and metallic boom rang out as all the panels chimed the gloomy bell of disaster.

But something weird happened. He appeared to go right through. I had to rub my eyes, trying to refocus and confirm what I was seeing.

Did he jump?

I didn't see him jump.

He must have gone right through, as if the panel was nothing but a mere hologram, and galloped himself back into his paddock with the gate left open (always to the inside of the paddock). I followed his path with an apprehensive, quiet and slow walk dreadfully looking for blood and body parts. To my relief, I found none.

I looked up and saw him standing at the end of his paddock close to the neighbouring horse, seeking comfort, with the end of the lead line behind him, free of his legs with no tangles. I picked up the end of the lead line and gently signaled him to look over his withers at me. He was breathing hard but seemed to be gradually calming down with each breath. Shockingly he looked happy and relieved to see me with a "Holy shit, what the hell was that?" expression on his face. He seemed to not have a clue what happened or how he got there. Only that something scared the crap out of him and he let instincts take over. RUN TO SAFETY!!! There didn't seem to have been much of a thought process beyond that. He was extremely light in his responses to my request to come over and let me examine him. I was expecting to see bone, torn flesh or dangling skin.

I couldn't find a single scratch on him.

In total disbelief I asked him to come with me back to the scene of the accident, just so the two of us could try to figure out how he got out.

During the walk back I couldn't detect any signs of lameness, which was amazing. Another thing I noticed, that I found equally amazing, was how light, cooperative and responsive he had become. He seemed eager to go back to check things out.

Examining his point of exit at the arena confirmed my suspicions. He hadn't jumped. He had gone right through the panel as if it were made of papier mâché. The sight of the panel was nothing short of terrifying. It elevated my respect for horse power to a whole new, hard to reach level. As amazed as I was by what I was seeing, what had just happened and the lack of a scratch on this hulk of a horse, I couldn't keep from thinking about how light and soft he felt at the end of the line. Something we had been struggling with for quite some time. I find warmbloods to be the most abrasive and hard headed breed of them all. But not now. Not this second. He'd done a 180 with a major break-through, pun intended!

The fence piece Marcelo went through, with a gator filled with shit in the background

I saw a window of opportunity that was not available to us before. A mental blockage had been removed through the literal obliteration of a fence panel, and the horse was now more than welcoming to the support and guidance he did not deem necessary or of much value before.

With zero doubt in our minds, we changed venue to the large, round indoor-arena. I mounted and together we moved and transitioned from one gait to another, up and down, left and right, forwards and backwards, smooth and effortless like flowing water. As one.

Of course all of this is credit to sheer dumb luck! He could have died. The fact that he hadn't gotten hurt was astronomical. Yes, we seized the moment and capitalized on something terrible, but that didn't change the fact that I had picked the wrong venue, the wrong geometrical space for the job.

Body Language and Intention

There is what seems like an infinite number of variables that will slightly change what I would like to call the "tone" or "volume" of the conversation or interaction with your horse.

Knowing and understanding how different spatial settings affect the conversations will guide us in choosing our "words" or "tone" more strategically, depending on the kind of space we are in.

I want to be careful about calling it a conversation. It is a conversation. But obviously not in the verbal manner we mean between humans. It is a symbiotic conversation that is based on universal body language that in itself is based on basic and fundamental laws of physics and therefore relatable to all that exists, sentient or not. For our purposes, it is important to draw a non-judgmental distinction between this definition of a conversation as opposed to what an Animal Communicator might mean, or perhaps to a more anthropomorphic understanding of a conversation.

Before we further examine which "tone" is appropriate and in line with the space we are interacting in, I need to clarify a little bit more about what I mean by "tone" expressed through body language.

There are many obvious physical manifestations that determine the "tone" of our body language. Speed, Muscular Tension, Breathing, Heart Rate all convey telling tales about our true state of mind and feelings often misrepresented by our verbal expressions.

Every day I try to become more aware of what tone is being expressed physically as opposed to verbally.

Is it hostile? Is it curious? Is it defensive? Is it offensive?

And not just an understanding of the horse's tone but also my own. What kind of tone is my body language conveying?

The tone is determined by our energy and the manner in which we move, which are greatly influenced by our true inner intentions that are not always consistent with our outward expressions.

It's interesting to see the incongruency in people's body language and verbal expressions.

One of the most common ones I see and hear is the horse handler using reassuring words to calm their horse down while their body and even the inflection of the words tell and communicate a completely different message, usually one that says "Oh my God, I'm so scared right now. Please don't hurt me." This, in turn, sends the opposite message to the horse, as all the horse hears and registers is a nervous tone and mannerism that expresses panic and fear, as opposed to calmness and reassurance from the handler.

But not only can the incongruency happen between the verbal and physical expressions, but also within the body itself. Maybe what our hands are saying and gesturing is not being followed through and supported by our stance, leg position or more importantly, our balance.

More often than not we are completely unaware of what our bodies are conveying as opposed to what we think we are putting out there.

Here's an example of what I'm talking about.

Fire – Human to Horse Communication

A non-horse savvy friend of mine was at our ranch in Aldergrove to help me put up some fences. The particular field we were working in was about three acres, housing four horses, one stallion and three geldings. At the top there was a gravelled area where the horses' feeder and shelter were located. Anything with gravel on it had to be picked. Before we could get started on repairing the fence the gravel area needed to be mucked.

My friend, Tony, decided to help me with the chores before tackling the old, broken fence. The horses were feeling social that day and hanging out close to us while we mucked around them.

Before long Tony ran into a problem.

The Arabian stallion named Fire was standing in a spot Tony was trying to pick and wouldn't move.

Tony turned to me and asked, "What do I do? This guy won't budge."

Puzzled as to why or how this was happening, I instructed him to wave his arms and try shooing him off.

Cluck.

Kiss.

Nothing.

Okay then maybe poke him with your pitchfork a bit.

Nope.

All the noise, gesturing and hubbub achieved nothing.

In fact it was obvious that the more Tony tried, the braver and more resilient Fire grew, and he was now thinking of expanding his territory right on top of Tony's head.

Of course all this was expressed clearly in the body language. Fire's balance of weight in his body was shifting to the front and his chest from the previous more neutral, grounded, mid-section position that was there prior to Tony's escalating efforts.

But let's not forget about Tony's balance and the placement of weight in his body. The entire time Tony was waving his arms, clucking and shooing, even poking with his pitchfork, his weight was tilting back in a retreating, defensive stance, as opposed to positioning his core with a slight tilt to the front in his chest for forward momentum.

To Fire nothing could be more obvious and telling.

Tony's body was yielding to Fire's awesome presence despite all the physical and verbal nonsense that was going on with his mouth, arms and even his plastic pitchfork. That's what Fire picked up on and that is what he was about to react to, perhaps not in such a gentle way.

Tony was in potential danger as Fire was fixing to show him how claiming space is done effectively.

He was about two feet from the stallion who was ready to show off with some dominant behaviour and posturing.

I scraped my boot on the gravel in an attempt to interrupt their interaction and steal Fire's attention for one second. That's all the time I needed.

From about fifteen feet away, I took one step towards Fire with my weight shifting into him using my outside hip and shoulder to express my intentions.

The space between us remained roughly the same.

Fire reacted immediately by rocking his weight from his chest back on to his hind. Took a couple of steps back, then moved his shoulder to the side and made way. The lateral move he performed was smooth and graceful as his front, no longer bearing all his weight, was light and agile. He looked magnificent.

"How did you do that??" asked Tony.

"Umm, I don't know" I answered. And I didn't really. I hadn't thought about it. I hadn't broken down the mechanics of it and intellectualized it. I had felt it, and experienced it, and just knew that it worked. The understanding of the mechanics of it and the science behind the behaviour would have to come much later.

Tony was gesturing a forward invasive move towards Fire, but the balance of his weight was in opposition to what he was trying to achieve and the stallion was not convinced. He wasn't buying it. Nobody was, including Tony, on a subconscious level. The balance in Tony's body was that of a person falling backwards, where mine was of a person gaining ground and barreling in. Short of ignoring Tony, Fire didn't really have a choice but to capitalize on the space being handed over to him.

This is not a problem exclusive to humans.

Horse to Horse Communication

Years later I was teaching a group lesson and we were watching two horses interact over the paddock fence. In one paddock we had a cool calm gelding standing in the immediate corner to his neighbouring paddock occupied by a hot headed, loud mouthed mare. The gelding was standing too close to the shared fence for her liking, infringing on her turf. She kept running at him, bearing her teeth, attempting to move him away from "her" fence. He was half asleep and would lazily blink an eye once in a while, completely ignoring her. All feet squared, with one hind foot cocked, swishing flies with his tail, the gelding had no intention of moving. He would barely look at her as she charged at him over the fence repeatedly. She was full of empty gestures. He knew it, she knew it, I knew it and I wanted my students to know it.

A split second before reaching the fence the balance in her body would shift from full on forward to a hesitant weak finish towards the back. She didn't mean business. My students blamed the fence. It was pointed out that obviously she couldn't follow through because of the physical barrier the fence provided.

I disagreed.

There was much more to it than the physical barrier. It was written all over her body and lack of commitment she disclosed at the very last second of her grandiose display of pretentious macho bravado. She reminded me of someone who is relying on their buddies to hold them back in a fight, so despite appearances they won't actually have to fight. I know it well as I've been there. Maybe you have too. The louder the bark the lesser the likelihood of an actual bite.

There was only one way to prove it. I had to move the gelding through and over the fence preferably without the need to make actual physical contact, but fully intending to, if necessary.

I got the gelding's attention by making some subtle noise, making sure he had noticed me and was registering my presence. A couple steps towards him with a swing of my lead line and he came to life in hurry and scooted right out of there. The corner was mine, and I was well over twenty feet away from him. We never came remotely close to making actual contact, because I meant it and he knew it, so I didn't have to prove it.

Yes the fence was there, but if the mare really meant business, she could have easily reached over and bitten him. He knew she wouldn't go there and couldn't care less about her empty threats. Her heart wasn't in it.

The shift of weight is one of the physical voicings that can give us a truthful and accurate outward expression of what is happening on the inside.

The opposite of this scenario also happens.

I have worked with horses whom I've asked to back up, only to have them move their feet in a backward motion, but never shift their weight to the hind, rather keeping their weight in the front while moving backwards. This is not a true back-up. Despite the backward movement of the feet, the horse is still leaning into me, pushing, and not truly yielding the space I was asking for. It's meaningless unless the shift of balance happens first. Then, and only then, do we have a true back up. A true yield.

If the true yield doesn't happen, you will find the horse pushing, coming back into that space over and over again as the claim to ownership has not quite been settled as far they're concerned. I call this "the yo-yo syndrome," where you see a handler needing to ask for space from the same horse over and over again. It's a frustrated physical manifestation of a nagging argument between two parties that never gets settled. It gets annoying and sours the time and experience between the two parties involved, as neither one is able to get resolution to the dispute and find peace. The matter should be settled in a black and white manner, with no grey areas of ambiguity and confusion. Only then can you move on and the relationship can grow, instead of plateauing over a relatively simple yet extremely important matter, space ownership.

Claiming Space - The Shit Picker's Perspective

Before we go any further, I think I need to make a little bit more sense of what I'm trying communicate, and explain the shit picker's perspective I have acquired when it comes to moving horses that entails another meaning and usage of spatial relations.

It's not about the horse. It's about the space. It's about the turf. Moving the horse is only consequential to claiming the space.

As we saw earlier with Tony, his intention or interest wasn't to move a horse per se. It was to gain access to a piece of turd on a piece of turf the horse was occupying.

This may seem confusing or silly, but I can't stress enough how important and essential this has been to my interactions in working around and with horses. Tony needed to gain access to a piece of real estate and he had a good reason for it. He needed to muck that spot. The stallion was challenging him on the ownership of this spot.

I find that important because it immediately takes me out of the frame of mind that intends to control or dominate the horse and shifts my perspective and intentions to claiming ownership of a piece of turf. The turf, not the horse. The horse may or may not challenge my claim. If he does, the second he concedes, the dispute is over and all goes back to a calm norm again. To me, this is the true meaning and idea behind the "Release" that many trainers talk about. It changes the psychology and dynamics between people and horses.

Of course, it's not just a competition or claim to ownership of turf. There's much more to it than that. But this is one of the fundamentals that needs to be established. The ownership of space is something that needs to be settled before a more sophisticated and complex relationship and partnership can begin to develop.

However, there is something else that precedes claiming ownership. For a horse the space must be defined and explained before we can proceed to the question of ownership. It makes perfect sense if we put it in words. Before you can claim to own something, you must have a clear idea of what that something is.

So before I can claim ownership of the space, I need to define the space.

Just recently at the Rock'n Star Ranch, in our new location in Pritchard, BC, we turned fifteen horses loose on a quarter section (160 acres). The first order of work for the horses was to check out the perimeter fence. During this process no horse challenged another. They moved together in harmony along the fence line and got a feel for the lay of the land. Once the spatial characteristic of the land was mapped out, they proceeded to determine who was in charge of the now-defined space. And only after the ownership was established did it become possible for them to move as a herd in a manner which would maximize survival and safety under the direction and trusted leadership of the designated horse in charge of the space.

There is great importance in the order of events.

As a direct result and out of sheer necessity for me to do my chores back in the stallion's field with Tony, Fire and I had come to a clear understanding and agreement as to who was in charge of the space.

I was.

This made it possible for us to move to the next level of our relationship and cohabitation: the dance and synchronicity between two bodies in a shared space.

Fire had decided I was ready for this next lesson.

The Tidal Dance

Fire was the first horse to teach me about the physical mechanics of body language and the interaction between two masses ruled by basic laws of physics and nature.

I will never forget the day he became my teacher.

It was about 7:30 am, on a crisp November morning. The ground felt hard from the freeze the previous night and my worst fears were confirmed. The shit was frozen to the ground. All the clues were there. The slight sting in my fingers, the resistance of the frost-jammed clip on the gate. But how bad? Would it come loose with my plastic pitch fork if I poked at it from the right angle? Or would it break the plastic fork and send me fetching the metal one? Judging from the ice formation on the trough I knew what to expect.

I remember thinking, "I should be indoors. I should be on stage. How in the hell did I end up here?" I had given up my cushy, union job at U.B.C. Theatre Department with good pay, summers off and hardly anything to do to work full time as a shit picker on a 20 acre equestrian facility in

Aldergrove, BC. Looking after a herd of horses. Trying to stay alive, every minute of the day around these half-ton beasts. It was beneath me, I thought, a monkey could do this job! I had a university degree and was a lead guitarist in a band that had just gotten signed to a label with Universal distribution! And here I was shoveling shit, why? Because the family business needed to move and expand from the original 3 acre place in Richmond, but primarily, I was told by my wife Christa, it was because Fire needed more space!

So there I was in the midst of an existential crisis, arguing with a stubborn, frozen piece of horse shit that would not budge, when I noticed the culprit himself, Fire, standing about three feet or so away from me, making eye contact and shifting and moving his body in relation to the movements I was making while mucking. It was like a dance that I was leading unbeknownst to me, until he pointed it out and showed me. If I shifted my weight back or stepped back he would move in accordingly and vice versa. The tone was calm, gentle and patient. There were no signs of dominance, hostility, competition for hierarchy or status.

It was my main eureka moment.

It was the moment I fully understood that this horse was connecting and communicating with me. Why he did that when the other three horses in there ignored me, I will never know. Perhaps because he was the top horse in the field and a representative of the other horses. Maybe it was something else. Whatever the reason, he deliberately came over to me that day to teach me something important. To clue me in to what I needed to know.

To what I needed.

It was no different than the interaction between a gentle breeze and the leaves in the trees. It just was. It was the simple dance of creating space and occupying space. As I vacate a space you fill the void and vice versa, connected together through a magnetic pull, a gravitational pull.

I was beginning to understand what moving together should feel like. A complete lack of bracing, pushing, shoving as two bodies willingly move together in harmony. A feeling that immediately induces endorphins and euphoria. This was the end goal. This was what I needed to look for and learn to create.

It was magical in the same way everything in nature is magical. In the same way gravity is magical, movement of tides, the changing of seasons. We are surrounded by it every day, but we are too distracted by fairy tales and stories concocted to suit and soothe our psychological needs and unacknowledged imbalances, to notice the real everyday wonder and miracles around us. We're not just surrounded by it; we are governed by it and it is un-wavered by our opinions, half-assed theories or ignorance.

It just is.

The language is real. But for the most part unused, ignored. Horses have learned or given up on trying to use it to communicate with us for a number of reasons.

One of the reasons, in this shit picker's humble opinion, is the incongruencies in our intentions and body language. A disconnect between actual reality and the perceived, edited notion we tell ourselves.

In a horse's eye, we say one thing and we do another. We ask for something and get mad or scared when they comply.

We don't do it on purpose.

It's the plight of our species.

From a young age we are conditioned to practice separating and compartmentalizing what we think with what we say. It's this well practiced disconnect between our true feelings and the attached meanings to the words we use to communicate that gets us in trouble.

The other aspect of it is how unaware we are of our own body postures and what they are conveying to the rest of the world. I don't know how many times I've watched someone, white-knuckling their rope, pulling their horse into them on line, only to get mad at them for crowding them.

Just think of how different you look in pictures or videos of yourself riding, as opposed to how thought you looked.

How Do I Look?

I remember being in a clinic with a very well respected and admired horseman friend of ours, Daryl Gibb. We all mounted our horses in the morning and Daryl was going to have quick chat before we hit the hills in Osoyoos, B.C. for a long trail ride. He asked "Does anybody have any questions?" To which I responded "Yes. How do I look?" To which everyone laughed. Daryl chuckled and said "You look good."

"Then I'm good to go," I said, ready to take on some challenges with my mare.

Yes, it was cheeky and humorous, but I strongly believe if things don't look good, or let's say "right" to use a less vain term, then they're not.

When you're sitting tall in your saddle with your body perfectly balanced and aligned, you look good! If your horse is balanced and moving using the proper muscles and self- carrying, your horse looks good. If something, anything, is off balance, things will look shitty, forced and awkward.

If you mean to do one thing but your body is doing another, that won't look good. It will look awkward and off.

So yeah. I want to know if I look good leading my horse. Is it effortless and fluid or are there signs of struggle and conflict? The same in the saddle. The same with my aids, the same with everything. Does it look balanced? Does it look fluid? Does it look effortless?

How do I look?

How do you look?

Through horses, I have become more self-aware. I have learned to police myself, my body, my balance, my mental state at all times. Am I calm? Am I rattled? Am I focused? Am I being honest? Am I being consistent in mind and body?

Ninety-nine percent of the time if our horse doesn't look or move right it's because of something we're doing wrong, and by that I mean off balance, physically and or psychologically. It's because somewhere along the way a disconnection between our mind and body has occurred that is in turn causing a disconnection between us and our horse.

Oh yeah! The horse! We can't forget about the other half of the equation here. Not only are we required to align within ourselves but we must now align with our horse. This can only happen through a two-way line of communication and exchange of information between horse and rider. A line of communication and dynamics that is primarily built on spatial relations, terms and conditions, before it grows into feel, signal and balance in the saddle.

But it has to start with us. I can't maintain balance in my horse if I can't create balance in myself first. Balance is of great importance to horses. A physically imbalanced horse is a prime target for predators. A psychologically imbalanced horse is a liability to the herd, usually spurned and therefore also prime target for predators. If I am off balance in the saddle I am compromising my horse's chances of survival by negatively affecting their balance. If I am off balance psychologically, perhaps the same.

I can't create anything in my horse unless I can create it in myself first.

If I want my horse to be calm, I must be calm. If I want my horse to be brave, I must be brave. If I want my horse to be patient, I must be patient. If I want my horse to be respectful, I must be respectful. If I want my horse to be kind, I must be kind. Think about what you want from your horse and ask yourself for it first.

Fire finding balance on the plank

A little R&R time with Fire on a trip to Kelowna

Fire exploring new obstacles at Twisted Terrain Park in Hope

Fire enjoying the view from the top of a mountain at Keremeos

2 WORKING AND LIVING SPACE

A shit picker's chores will press spatial awareness to the forefront of our interactions with horses at all times in a variety of manifestations.

At the Aldergrove ranch, 20 acres, we had a variety of spatial settings with the horses.

We had stalls that we used for injured horses or ones that needed special care and needed restricted movements.

Then we had three types of paddocks. The regular paddocks were 20x40 single occupancy with a shelter and feed box. Then there were double size paddocks at 40x40, some set up for single occupancy and some for two horse occupancy with two feeders and split shelter for each horse.

In addition we had shared field boarding. We limited and determined the number of the horses living in each field based on the size of the field. Each field was outfitted with a gravel area that had their shelters and feeders on it, and an open range area that provided seasonal grazing with room to gallop and horse around.

We also had four fenced grazing pastures that we rotated the paddock horses in, so they had a chance to graze and stretch their legs and wouldn't be confined to the paddocks 24/7. Sometimes these grazing fields would host cattle for short periods of time.

Each one of these housing options presented its own set of challenges, quirks and lessons from the horses that lived in them.

The number one tool I used for getting all my chores done was the mighty John Deere gator. It was a simple two wheel drive TS model with hydraulic dumper. Our square hay bales were from Washington and weighed about 110 lbs on average. The gator was the perfect vehicle to get these bales around. I would stack around four bales per trip in the bed of the gator. And I did all the mucking with the gator as well.

The paddocks

Grazing/playing fields

Tie stalls

The Oval

The gator (Chillie driving)

Defining Space

Whether it was delivering hay or mucking, I would drive the gator right into the paddocks to get the job done. The gates were 10 footers, and the challenge was to get out of the gator, open the gate, get back in the gator, drive the gator in, jump back out and close the gate behind me before the horse ran out. Paddock horses were always very motivated to get out as there was grass they'd been eyeing just few strides away from each gate, not to mention other horses to visit in various fields spread out over the entire property.

In order not to let a horse out, I had to develop an understanding for drive lines and application of pressure.

For the purposes of simplifying the matter, we will talk about three main drive lines on the horse's body. For our first line, imagine a vertical line drawn from the tip of the horse's nose down to the ground. The second line is in the mid-section and the third is behind the tail. The position the pressure comes from towards the lines will determine the direction in which the horse is going to move.

For example, if I am standing ahead of the horse and therefore ahead of first drive line and I apply pressure, that is going to create a backup from my horse. If I am behind the said drive line and I apply pressure it will cause a forward motion from my horse.

So coming in with the gator I had to make sure to stay ahead of the drive line if I wanted my horse to back up and away from the gate.

If the horse didn't respond to the pressure to move back and I continued to advance without a pause, and didn't wait for the right movement to happen, I would end up behind the drive line and the pressure would move the horse forwards, past me and out the open gate.

The pressure, I might add, is almost never actual contact, but a wave of the arm, swing of the rope, a pointed pitchfork, or gesturing at the drive line on the horse with energy and proper shift of balance in your body. It's pretty hard to apply direct pressure from the driver's seat of the gator.

Through this system the end result looked something like this.

I would drive up to the gate, adjacent to the feeder, where the horse would be standing and eating. I would swing the gate open to the inside of the paddock, get back in the gator and proceed slowly into the paddock with subtle hand gestures applying pressure to the front drive line of the horse. The horse would back up in synch with the slow speed of the gator. All the while I would maintain the pressure ahead of the drive line, making sure I didn't move past it and cause a forward motion out of the horse, sending her out the open gate. Once I had cleared the length of the gate, I would stop, get out and close it behind me, while the horse stood beyond an invisible line in front but to the side of the gator, leaving a path open in front of him. It was important that the gator did not obstruct the horse during this process. Using the gator as a physical means to block and push the horse in the paddock would have most horses in a panic, feeling trapped and desperately seeking an escape from the machine, triggering their flight instincts.

Now I could pick the paddock, leave the horse alone, only moving him if he was in my way of getting to a shit pile.

This was a much higher level of challenge and effectiveness in moving my horse, since I was not only dealing with an open gate, but I also had to get my horse to yield and leave her manger in order for me to do what I needed done in the paddock.

By the time I had this much understanding, practical usage of the drive lines and precision application of pressure, working a horse in the round pen seemed incredibly elementary and easy.

Of course getting a handle on all this did not happen overnight. It started with the subtle lessons learned from Fire.

It started with an understanding of the basic principles of movement in relation to pressure and space. I had to learn how to do it without the gator first, without an open gate.

I had the privilege of practicing these principles and exercises with over thirty horses on a daily basis in different spatial settings. Each one slightly different from the other, I had to learn how to adjust my energy and pressure and customize my "ask" to the individual horse. The amount of pressure that it would take to move one horse would be way too much for another, or not nearly enough for the sensitivity level and response of the next.

The other incredibly valuable opportunity in a shit picker's day presented to me was feeding.

Feeding provided a great setting for lessons in establishing boundaries and food etiquette with my horses.

Bringing hay into the paddock would require the same strategy for driving the gator in, in order to deposit 110 lb bales into our wooden feeders for 24/7 access to hay. The feeders were outfitted with hockey nets mostly to keep the hay inside the feeders and prevent waste. I don't think the size of the holes were small enough for this feature to offer "trickle" feeding for the horses.

Pinto delivering hay in the gator

A quick side note, I'm not a big fan of "trickle feeding." I find if the horses are struggling and having a hard time getting their hay out, it puts them in a rotten mood and leaves them more temperamental to deal with when training and riding. I think the holes in the net should be small enough to keep the hay from spilling and going to waste, but wide enough so that the horses can pull out a mouthful without a lot of hassle.

Happy horse, happy ride.

For the most part, the majority of the horses I've looked after over the years self-regulate their consumption to the correct amount, relative to their weight, size and workload. A very rough number I have in mind in general is about 1 lb of hay per hour for the average horse.

If a horse failed to self-regulate to a healthy amount, we would cut back on the amount of hay we gave them access to. This would hardly ever happen. But it did happen from time to time.

Anyways I digress. That will happen a lot. Like I said, we're trying to tackle a three dimensional topic in a one dimensional format. So . . . sorry.

Where were we? Right! Feeding with the gator.

Feeding hay required the same strategy of getting the gator through the gate of the paddock without losing the horse, plus the added challenge of now having hay in the gator. Many horses would get pushy and antsy during this process and found what I required from them in order for me to able to get the hay in the feeder quite challenging.

They needed to stand quietly at a distance in the paddock while I lifted the bale out of the back of the gator, into the feeder, clipped the net back over the new bale, cut the strings, walked back to the gator, and backed out of the still open gate, before they were finally allowed to walk back to the feeder, in a calm orderly manner, and eat.

The reason why it needed to be done in this manner was purely for practical and functional reasons. Anything less could have resulted in disaster. Maybe not today, but tomorrow. Maybe not this paddock, but the next.

You don't have time to argue or the opportunity to horse around when you're lifting a 110 lb bale and putting it in the feeder. You must ask for plenty of space and insist not to be rushed or harassed by your horse while you're trying to get the task done. I realized once I was successful in keeping the horse at bay, standing quietly and patiently, I didn't have to close the gate behind me anymore. And that saved me time and additional hassle in getting the hay out. For 30+ horses, we're looking at 3300 lbs of hay going out every feeding cycle. So shaving a little time off here and there added to a lot at the end of the day.

Also, if I can get a horse to stand quietly and patiently at the end of the paddock while I do what I need to do, then having a horse stand quietly on line was a cinch.

Think about how many horses push and shove, dance around and hassle the handler when being asked to stand still for a minute while you have conversation with a fellow equestrian. Once you learn to do this, you will have a quiet horse who will stand there still and not budge for as long as you want to gossip with your friend, text, smell the flowers, pet a dog. Oh the possibilities!!

However, the benefits can reach much further than that.

Here's one small example.

Lily, the Moody Tacker

I was called to a friend's place to do an assessment on a horse who was acting a bit aggressive during tacking up, biting and threatening to kick.

Lily, an off the track Standardbred, lived in a large paddock with a big shelter she shared with a small pony and a quarter horse mare. The horses were out grazing when the owner, Melissa, corralled them back into the large paddock area. I was leaning against the fence, inside the paddock with my arms stretched out, resting on the top rails, watching and taking notes not only of Lily's dynamics with the other horses, but also with Melissa as well.

Lily was the top mare, no doubts about it. As the three horses went past me towards the shelter in the corner, Lily shot me a really nasty look that said "Who the hell let you in here?" I noticed she slightly threw her hind into my direction as fair warning that she wasn't afraid to kick me if she had to. The look she gave me was so nasty that even Melissa noticed it from a distance.

"Holy crap did you see that?" I commented. If looks could kill, I'd be dead, and if I verbalized the body language it would have been filled with four letter words. "Wow, she cusses like a sailor!" I told Melissa.

We had a good laugh about that.

Melissa haltered a stiff necked, stiff lipped Lily and brought her over to the hitching post located inside the paddock. "Now what?" she asked. "Well, do what you normally do and I'll watch. See what I can see. Usually tacking issues are due to some kind of physical discomfort, be it an ill-fitting saddle, sore back, ulcers, something like that. I don't know. We need to figure out if the source of the misbehaviour is pain related or just attitude," I said.

Melissa began grooming Lily and prepping her for the saddle. Signs of aggression were already starting to emerge during this process. Ears were pinning and she was threatening to nip, without full commitment at this stage.

The manner and tone with which the horse was objecting to grooming didn't correspond at all to a horse who was experiencing physical pain or discomfort. I took over the grooming to see if I could detect any sore spots on Lily's back by applying gentle pressure. I couldn't find any as she was non-reactive.

It all felt like a space ownership issue more than anything else. It seemed consistent within the context of what she had shown us coming into the paddock earlier. She was clearly the top mare and that position was not limited to horses but people too. It was only a theory, so we decided to run an experiment and let Lily tell us if we were right or wrong.

I asked Melissa to run me through the morning routine. "What happens first thing in the morning?"

"Well, I come up to her paddock with the wheelbarrow of hay and I toss it over the wall," she said.

"Okay, let's stop right there and address that. If we run into a problem, we'll work on it. If not, we'll move on to the next step," I suggested.

Instead of tossing the hay over the half wall of the shelter, I decided to bring the flakes in and ask for space while I placed them in the manger.

Of course, Lily was all over me and I had to put some work into claiming the space and hay. It took some convincing to get her to back off and wait before being allowed to eat. It was a hard pill for her to swallow, being told what to do on her turf as the queen of the castle.

We concentrated on working on space ownership. Once that was settled, we further solidified matters by asking Lily to leave the hay when asked.

This is something I've seen the top horses do in a herd situation. If you have a number of horses and you lay out flakes in various spots for the herd to eat, you will notice the top horse go from pile to pile, moving the other horses off before she/he settles down to a specific pile. It's not about being greedy and wanting all the hay, it's about confirming who is in charge.

It was a bit of work, but before long, Lily got with the new program. Once I was able to do it, I asked Melissa to take over and do the same thing a few times, letting Lily know she's not in charge of the space and hay, we are. After a little break we haltered her back up to see if this new arrangement had changed anything about the grooming and tacking process. To our surprise it had. The biting, protesting and acting up all disappeared. Lily now stood quietly and relaxed while being groomed and saddled. She seemed content to allow us access to her body parts for grooming and tacking purposes, no longer threatening to bite, with relaxed ears and stance. Furthermore, this improved things greatly in the saddle when it came to following the feel and yielding to the aids. But that's another story.

Owning the Space

Fields and Shark Tanks

Food aggression can lead to serious problems with safety around horses. Feeding etiquette is a must as far as I'm concerned and can prevent disastrous accidents from occurring.

I got called into another ranch with a horse that had become food aggressive. This was a youth guest ranch with generally quiet, experienced horses that had become pretty dull and spoiled through some mishandling they got from young beginner riders. The wranglers there informed me that over time this particular gelding had become quite dangerous during feeding. It started out with subtle and small signs of protest if someone was in his space, to a full-on double barreling out if you were within ten feet of him while he was eating. This horse took a lot more work than Lily.

I decided to start discussing space ownership with him on line. Maybe that was a mistake. Maybe it would have been easier, better and safer in a liberty setting, but that wasn't available to us at this particular ranch set up. I remember him getting quite physical and abrasive during this session, charging, trying to bite, kicking and pawing, fighting hard to maintain ownership of the turf around him. This went on for almost two hours. I was sweating and scared as he had gotten quite bold about laying into people and getting them to back down by acting aggressively. But we got through it and he finally started yielding ownership of the space. Once things felt good on line, we introduced grain and hay to the scenario and worked on him yielding and leaving his food on command from all directions, e.g., at his shoulders, from behind and front.

After a total of three hours of excruciating work, the horse was finally at peace and safe to be around while he was eating. We were able to ask him to leave even the grain without him protesting or displaying aggression.

The wranglers jokingly said okay, we got few dozen more out there. I said alright, let's see what we can do. They thought I was joking. But I wasn't.

Here's the routine they were following. The horses were in a large field and come feeding time the wranglers would swing the gates open and jump out of the way as the horses stampeded into the barn to the tie stalls with hay and grain waiting for them in the feeders. The stampede was wild and unruly, and was getting worse by the day. Some of the newer wranglers felt compromised and unsafe. The more experienced ones didn't seem too concerned, but were not particularly against things mellowing out a bit.

I was already exhausted from the three hour session with the one horse and didn't have a lot more gas left in me, so I had to do something quick, effective and in an energy efficient manner.

I had learned a lot from feeding the horses in our fields in the previous years, so before I tell the rest of the story I will take you through the details of what I had to deal with at our place first.

Operating in the Oval

One particular field we had was called The Oval. It housed seven mares. My job was to drive the gator up to the gate with three bales of hay for an anticipating herd of excited mares. Park. Get out. Swing gate open. Get back in. Drive the gator through the gate. Get back out. Close the gate. Get back in the gator and drive it through the field to the feeders. All the while trying to manage seven horses not only from not running out the gate, but giving me enough space and time to get back into the gator safely.

That was just half the job.

The only way for me to do this safely was to establish ownership of the space around me. A space that travelled with me and was constant. It wasn't a designated spot. It wasn't the gate itself or a fence line. The space had to be defined and explained to the horses in relation to where I was, in relation to my body, wherever it happened to be.

I had to establish a circle with at least a twenty foot radius around me that no horse was allowed in, unless invited.

No one taught me how to do this. Actually that's not accurate. No human taught me how to do this. The horses did. It was a matter of getting the job done and the horses let me know what was working and what was not, the hard way!!

Once you have had to chase and corral a bunch of loose horses on twenty acres back to their field when it's dark, cold and wet, you get really serious and creative about figuring out how to do things right and avoid disaster.

Establishing the space I needed was experimental. I had to figure out how to get the horses out of my space. It wasn't easy. I would push two horses out on the right, only to have another three move in from the left. I can only imagine how ridiculous and comical all this must have looked and sounded day after day, while I tried to figure this shit out. Through much trial and error, I finally sorted it out.

It was so simple, it was stupid!

Manage the top, boss mare and the herd will follow. She's the only one I really had to deal with. She spoke for the rest of the herd. Can we call this the "take me to your leader" or "I'd like to speak to the manager" technique? (Extreme haircuts not required).

With that in that mind, let's get back to the story of the unruly mob of horses at the other ranch.

Meanwhile, Back at the (Youth) Ranch

With just a lead line I approached the gate. There were four lead horses in this group and it was clear who they were. None of the rest of the herd would dare approach the gate before or ahead of these guys come feeding time. They were the first ones to go through and the first to reach their tie stalls and eat.

Alright. Our problem just shrank from dealing with the whole herd of horses to dealing with only these four. Not bad. It only took seconds to determine that.

The top four started advancing towards the gate immediately when they noticed me approaching. I started swinging my rope and claiming space right there and then while still at least twenty feet away from the gate. They were a bit shocked. That was not standard procedure and I was not someone they recognized to boot. Experiencing pressure to move through and over closed gate and fences was strange to them. It was unusual. "People" don't normally do that.

I got them stopped in their tracks and was able to keep them at bay while I cracked the gate open and took my spot on the inside of the field, claiming it, owning it.

And so the testing of the waters began. Cautiously, the top four horses tried to figure out how close they could get to me before I reacted and pushed them back out. I kept them at about a twenty foot distance. Charged them a few times. Bit a couple of them hard with the end of my rope on the rump, as I chased them back and released pressure the second the space I wanted was given. The space was mine and the gate was in it. It took maybe about ten minutes until the matter felt settled. No more challenges, no more testing and no more doubt in their mind that I owned that space.

Next came the moment of truth.

I told the wranglers I was going to swing the gate open and didn't expect any horse to run through the gate as long as I was standing there.

It was a big risk.

I swung the gate open muttering a last prayer and hoped for the best. If it hadn't worked, I wouldn't be here today telling you this story.

The herd stood still knowing they were not allowed to approach until invited. This was the first step towards slowing things down to a safe pace.

I usually refer to this as "owning the gate." But that's not what it really is. It's owning the space and everything that happens to be in it. Be it the gate, the gator, tractor, wheelbarrow, hay, another horse . . . whatever.

Back at home I not only had to "own the gate" but also the gator and the hay. Otherwise the horses would be all over the gator fighting and kicking at each other while I'm manning the gate. Good luck trying to get back in there without getting hurt, past seven rival mares battling for ownership of the gator full of hay!

If the space is defined, the ownership established, a seemingly impossible task becomes not only possible, but easy and safe.

The same basic principle was at work for the completion of the feeding process which entailed driving the hay over to the feeders and putting the hay in them while maintaining and managing my space. Free of crowding and the dangers of horses competing for food with me caught in the middle or feeling like I'm swimming in a shark tank.

The Responsibility of Owning Space

As far as I'm concerned I owe my life to the understanding and the implementation of space ownership.

There's been plenty of occasions where I'd be fixing a net in a feeder standing shoulder to shoulder on the left side of a horse when another horse would come challenging that horse from the right. If my ownership of space was not well established, the horse beside me would move in a hurry into my space, trying to avoid the aggressor attacking from the right, knocking me to the ground and possibly trampling me, in an attempt to escape the other horse's hostile advance over hay. However, with the ownership of the space well established, this horse would not see my space as an available escape route and would choose a straight backup as the only available exit, rather than going through and over me.

But here's where we could take it to the next level. If I've really established my space concretely, the other horse would never bother or challenge a horse within my range of space to begin with.

I observed this type of dynamics in the herd often and decided to emulate and employ it to my advantage. In the herd the leader would never allow another horse to attack, address or mess with, in any way shape or form, a horse or horses under her care and protection. So with my space defined and owned, not only was any object (gator, gate, etc.) under my care and protection, but so was any sentient being including horses. A horse that was allowed and invited into my space would be under my protection and shielded from other horses, people, dogs, etc.

Now this is something to get excited about. One of the most common challenges we deal with is helping our horse to remain calm and unaffected by other horses. Especially when we are out riding the trails with other horses and riders coming and going. You may have noticed your horse becoming bothered with other horses entering or leaving the arena or various versions of the "herd bound" problems.

But how?? How can shit picking help us with these issues?

Lessons learned about space ownership while doing chores have come in quite handy in dealing with these problems.

I talked about my space and the protection the included horse enjoys within it. What does this do for the horse under my care?

Here's the long answer to that question.

Qualifying to Protect the Space

With the ownership of space comes a tremendous amount of responsibility.

Whenever I start working with a horse I always view it as applying for a job. A very important job. A job that lives depend on. So the job interview begins and the horse will need to be convinced that I am qualified for the position I'm applying for.

The first step is defining the space. The next step is determining the ownership of the space. Once these two items are settled the horse will need to make a decision on whether they are invited, included and protected in the said space by the one who owns it. The horse will be choosy as to whether they will trust their lives in the hands of the owner of this space and will require to see certain characteristics and capabilities from you, the owner of the space, in order to feel comfortable and safe, knowing you're reliable. The horse needs to be able to trust you with his life in your hands.

I've watched this process between horses numerous times. Some horses are able to establish ownership of space but not trust. These horses are usually too aggressive and though other horses will yield the space to them they will not share the space or form a bond. These aggressive horses stand alone and don't enjoy the benefit of living with the herd because the other horses see them as a threat not protection.

An analogy that I've found helpful is the dynamics between a pilot and his passengers. We need to know that our pilot is not only capable of flying the plane but has a vested interest in our safety and comfort. We want an experienced, confident pilot who will make all the right decisions and keep calm under pressure and emergencies, capable of making smart, well-informed, well thought-out decisions that will optimize our chances of survival and safety. With our trust in the pilot, we are able to relax and enjoy the flight without any concerns about our altitude, direction or any of the other huge responsibilities and work that comes with flying the plane. We need our pilot to be in charge in order to feel safe.

The black and white clarity of who is in charge is crucial to our feeling safe on the plane. Imagine how horrifying it would be if you heard the pilot announce, "Ladies and Gentlemen, this is your Captain speaking;

at this point I would like to consult you in making the decision regarding our altitude and route to the destination." I would immediately fear for my life knowing I'm several thousand feet up in the air with a pilot who doesn't know what the hell he's doing. This is not the time or place for ambiguity as to who is in charge!

A qualified, capable leader is able to decisively assume charge and create a secure environment for their horse, where the horse can relax and feel free of the responsibilities of keeping themselves from becoming prey. That's our job now. We are the ones carrying all the weight. They can relax and trust us to make all the right decisions as we do with our pilot when flying.

This trust is not to be taken for granted once it is earned. Anything and everything a horse gives us is a gift, even if we earn it. We must continue to maintain their trust by consistently making the right decisions that optimize survival and comfort. One reckless move from our pilot and all our trust vanishes immediately. The same applies to how our horse feels about us taking the controls. Just as with our pilot, our horses can lose trust in us by making a decision that compromises their safety and comfort.

However, this analogy falls short in some respects.

We must remember that horses are masters of survival and the bar is set very high for us to qualify in becoming a trusted leader, especially considering we can't see, smell or hear nearly as well as they do. As sentient beings that are no longer prey, our skills at survival in the wild are not nearly as sharp and well-practiced as horses. So why should a horse ever trust us enough to put their lives in our hands?

The Horse's Perspective

In trying to understand the horse's perspective when I'm applying for the leadership position, I had to think of a scenario where I would be putting my trust and life in the hands of someone less qualified than me. The pilot analogy does not quite capture the entirety of this scenario unless you are an expert in aviation, but I thought of one that did.

Teaching my daughter how to drive!!

Sitting in the passenger seat while my "just got my learners" teenaged daughter takes the wheel, and with it our lives, into her amateur, shaky, doubtful hands with an "I'm always right" teenage attitude, is a scenario that fits our purposes almost perfectly.

I remember how compromised and nervous I felt, thinking this must be how our horse feels at the end of the lead line attached to a human who does not know what the hell they're doing.

I found myself acting anxious, fidgety, nervous, trying to somehow gain back control of the travelling tin can we were trapped in.

I realized how easy it was to lose trust with every late stop, forgotten turn signal, hasty shoulder check, abrupt use of the gas pedal, jerky sharp hits on the brakes, lack of understanding of basic laws of physics when entering and coming out of a corner or sharp turn, driving too close to the curb in fear of being too close to the on-coming passing traffic, all coming from just a general lack of experience, awareness, confidence and control.

You can now see how a lack of control in our driver directly results in us fearing for our lives.

This is how our horses feel when we lack control. This is how compromised they feel when we halter or bridle them without knowing what we're doing.

Getting to know our equipment becomes another essential prerequisite in necessary qualifications.

When I first started, I constantly handled my lead rope, swinging, throwing and reeling it back up over and over again to have it become an extension of my body. Practiced handling a saddle relentlessly, putting on a halter or bridle without fumbling and goofing around, and handling my reins with dexterity. Horses notice these things and take notes. They see us coming miles away and we are less likely to win their confidence and "get the job" and win their trust if we're unfamiliar with the tools.

With the three main ingredients in place, definition of space, ownership of space and qualifying as protector of the space, our horse can feel secure, calm and unaffected by the world outside the secured bubble, as long as we continue to do a diligent job of guarding the space and the horse in it from threats, be they other horses, predators, plastic bags or yellow gum boots!

Competence, Not Dominance

Looking at things from this perspective, it becomes quite obvious that true leadership is about *Competence* not *Dominance*.

Our pilot does not win our trust and compliance to the rules of safety by dominating us, but by winning our confidence in her capabilities and skills. Nor can she bribe us into feeling confident and safe by offering us food, drinks and peanuts or telling us over and over again how much she loves us while brushing our hair.

I see a lot of people struggle with this concept. Domination and bribery fail equally in winning our horse's trust in our capabilities. At the end of the day, both extremes are used to compensate for a lack of skills in horsemanship.

My daughter only stands to win and maintain my trust by proving it to me every second she's in the driver's seat through exhibiting skills and good decision making, not by acting like a bully or by appealing to my affection for her while she veers towards the sidewalk!

What is reasonable for her to ask of me, however, is for some patience and the benefit of the doubt, which is exactly what I ask of my horses while I try to improve the skills required for the job I have taken on.

It's not about how we feel about each other on a personal level. My lack of trust in my daughter's skills behind the wheel are by no means indicative of how much I love her. They are a direct result of her lack of experience in driving and handling a vehicle. The less fumbling she does, the better I feel about trusting her to take charge of the controls in the vehicle.

Knowing that survival is the number one priority for my horse makes competent leadership a much more concrete base and foundation for our relationship to be built on than anything else. It's a much more difficult foundation to establish as it requires daily proof and maintenance and is something that is constantly under check and never taken for granted by the horse.

My dad was an excellent driver. Growing up I remember him being able to pull some pretty fancy moves in times of danger to keep us safe and prevent collision in situations caused by other drivers on the road. I never worried about my safety with my dad behind the wheel. But over the past years with him getting older I don't feel safe in the passenger seat anymore. He's a bit confused, indecisive and less confident. And just like that, a lifetime of trust disappeared through just a few mild signs of incompetence behind the wheel. One or two questionable decisions and I don't want to be in his car anymore.

Similarly your horse could just as easily and quickly lose confidence in you even after years of stellar track records. I see this in the herd all the time - positions change quickly if the leader of the herd is no longer fulfilling their duties proficiently, perhaps due to age or injury.

On the flip side of the coin, I've also noticed that horses in general are more patient than most people, and give us many more chances than I would when feeling compromised. They are dedicated teachers who don't seem to give up that easily on their dumb ass students.

Lyric

I've always found it fascinating how horses can become dangerous if they discover that people will back off and unintentionally provide release of aid and pressure if intimidated. Lyric was just such a horse.

Lyric was a three-year-old filly mix (Paint, Arab, Morgan, I'm not really sure) who had learned, through some round pen sessions with another handler, that people can be backed off with some macho attitude and aggressive display of horse power.

Not my horse, not my problem, I thought until it came to feeding time.

Lyric doing a 360° turn on the turn-around box

I went into her paddock one day to feed and asked her to back off and give me some room so I could put the flakes in the feeder without her breathing down my neck. She didn't like that, and came at me. I quickly dropped the flakes and tried to stand my ground. She wasn't buying it. Without a rope and with only my bare hands, I realized I was in a bit of a pickle. I didn't have much of a follow through with my threats and she was more than ready for the real deal as opposed to just posturing. I clapped my hands hard and threw them up at her palms out. This made her flinch a little and rocked her weight back some, just enough for me to be able to kick some sand up at her face for my follow through, which made her take two steps backs. I used that as my window of opportunity to reach for my lead line, the kind with leather poppers at the end, sitting just outside the paddock gate. Going back in with the rope swinging, she was easy to back off and got out of my space without much argument. The transformation in her was instant and significant. She immediately relaxed her top line and lowered her head, licking and chewing.

I wasn't at all interested in working with her, I just wanted to give her hay without her crowding me, but the change in her was so exaggerated that I got seduced into wanting to spend more time with this mare.

We continued our conversations about space ownership in the round pen.

Lyric was more than happy to let someone else be in charge of the space, as at her young age, she found the responsibility far too stressful and overwhelming. This is what may have contributed to her aggressive behaviour, stemming from insecurity.

It was a really easy job interview that mainly hinged on me demonstrating confidence in maintaining boundaries and shouldering the responsibilities of taking charge.

Once I passed that test Lyric was more than happy and willing to follow my lead and trust that I could keep us safe.

We were off to the races and progressing quickly. Within a week we were out of the arena and running around the acreage, doing chores, playing with various obstacles and challenges that were quite advanced for the short time we'd been at it. She confidently and enthusiastically

gave me whatever I asked for.

At that time Lyric was in a paddock being fed meals as I had not yet started giving the horses 24/7 access to the hay. In her particular case, this method of feeding proved disastrous. Lyric, still teething, had taken to gnawing on a piece of 2x6 in the shelter of her paddock every time she ran out of hay. This lead to a pretty extreme impaction colic as she ended up eventually devouring the whole 2 foot long piece!

The vet was called and regular treatments began with oil flushes and painkillers to no avail. The only option left for her now was costly surgery with no guarantees of success. Given that was not an option financially, the vet said, "Well if you keep her walking every couple hours for half hour or so the movement might help move things along."

I was determined to give it all I had, so I moved Lyric to one of the fields where she had access to fresh grass and could lie down more comfortably with less risk of injury. I parked the Living Quarter trailer by her field and took her for walks.

Every two hours.

Day and night.

During every walk she would pass a little dime size nugget. That was my only beacon of hope and motivation for the next walk. A whole week went by and I was getting really tired. Exhausted, with no sleep, I was losing hope and spirit. We were approaching the end of the second week with no major progress and it was starting to look like the only humane option left was to put her down. She had endured and suffered through much pain and discomfort for a very long time.

Finally, at the end of the second week, the impaction passed and she crapped twenty piles in a matter of hours. I had never been so happy to see horseshit in my entire shit picking life! Tears of joy uncontrollably streamed down my face.

After a few day's rest, like an idiot, I assumed all was well again and we had to make up for some lost time in our training. I wanted to pick up where we left off and stay the course as fast as we had been progressing.

Lyric had lost a lot of weight during the ordeal and the saddle was not fitting her like it did before. But I didn't take that into account and put her right back to work. She had been showing me subtle signs of discomfort that I brushed off and pressed on. She had started feeling different, no longer welcoming to the touch. Her responses to the contact started feeling evasive.

I kept pressing her, believing that she just needed to get pushed through it and, once she got moving and I put some miles on her, she would be fine.

So I decided to take her to a clinic our friend Daryl was having for some long rides in the hills of Osoyoos with a group of riders.

Lyric on the open range ride before meltdown

Lyric kept it together the first day, but by the second day, she started showing signs of discomfort early in the ride. She put up a fight going through the slip wire gate that gave us access to the hills, refusing to move forward and rearing a little bit. I just pushed her through it with a smile on my face, thinking she was just horsing around and being cute. We rode through the gate and started climbing the hills. We reached the top in a couple of hours where we dismounted, enjoyed the scenery and socialized with fellow riders, while giving the horses a chance to rest. Lyric was sweaty and looking spent, broken. On the way back, she couldn't take it anymore and started bucking downhill. The saddle was riding right up her neck and we were at the verge of disaster. So, finally recognizing the problem, I dismounted and lead her the rest of the way down the hill and got back on when the ground levelled out. It took me that long to finally listen to her that the saddle didn't fit her anymore and was hurting her.

When we got back home, feeling terrible and wanting to prove to her I had listened, I found her a better fitting saddle and took her to the covered, round arena. I still believed that with a better fitting saddle, all she needed to do was to move out, find her feet and get her confidence back.

I was wrong, again.

After warming up a bit on the ground and in the saddle, I asked her up to a canter. She picked it up and with every round we made she got faster and faster trying to run out from underneath me. So I dropped the reins and let her go. "Let her run and get it out of her system. What's the worst that can happen?" I thought.

Well, I found out the hard way.

The faster she got the more scared and insecure she became, until she finally lost her footing and tripped. We both went down crashing and tumbling. As she went head over heels, she put one foot on my hip then the other at my head, luckily I had my arm up and my elbow buffered and protected my skull. Another hoof landed on my right foot which she used as a springboard to get back up on her feet. I was winded and confused. I couldn't breathe or move. But I needed to see how Lyric was doing. After a while I got myself up to my knees and looked up. She was standing there terrified breathing hard with blood all over her. Her feet had clipped the inside of her legs and skinned them making the whole thing look like a scene out of Stephen King's *Carrie*.

I finally caught my breath and got up on my feet. I seemed to be okay. I walked over to her and examined her. She seemed alright besides the skinning. No apparent lameness, no broken bones. So, again, like an idiot, I got back in the saddle with the thoughts that I didn't want to leave things on a bad note. But what I didn't know at the time was that getting back in the saddle and moving my horse around didn't necessarily and automatically create a good note to leave on. Comforting her and calming her down would have gone much further in helping us leave on a better note.

Instead, I got on a bothered, frightened and bloodied horse and pushed her around some more which only resulted in her losing even more confidence in me and my ability to make good decisions. Not only did that make her feel compromised but it also send a clear message that the job was no longer about prioritizing her safety, but just doing what she was told. It took me a long time of reflecting to finally understand this and the severity of damage it causes to partnership.

Thankfully my pinky toe had broken where she used my foot as a springboard to get back up. If it hadn't it is possible that I wouldn't have spent the time reflecting on this situation at all and just brushed it off and carried on without learning anything from the experience.

I felt horribly responsible for what had happened to Lyric and needed to put the focus back on caring for and protecting my partner as opposed to chasing a "trainer's dream" of turning out a performance horse to feed my ego. So with that in mind, Lyric's weight loss became a point of focus for me.

I discussed the matter with our vet and he clued me in that the long term ordeal she went through with the colic has most likely wreaked all kinds of havoc on her intestinal system. A point I had never considered. I was just so glad she had "made it" that the aftermath of such an event never crossed my mind.

Not being able to eat properly for the entire duration of her colic had caused the acids in her stomach to do some damage.

We started by treating her for ulcers, with very fast and positive results. She started gaining weight quite rapidly but had a bad case of the runs. After seeking more advice and research, I put her on some pre- and probiotics to remedy any kind of hind gut issues she may have had. This too worked really well and her shit started looking healthy in no time.

Lyric was bouncing back. She'd put on a couple hundred pounds and was feeling like her old self again, so I decided to get back to some really easy, light ground work, on and off line.

It went incredibly well and soon we were back in the saddle doing everything we used to do. She was a little bit more apprehensive but pretty much the same horse I knew before all the shit hit the fan.

We got back into playing with obstacles, a hoof ball (a large 40" ball designed for horses to kick and push around), and a garrocha pole (a twelve foot long pole, traditionally used by Spaniards to handle cattle) until we ran out of challenges.

Lyric assisting in training another horse in the very same indoor where we had crashed a few months earlier

Instead of giving her a break and just being happy with what we had, I went back to trying to up the ante every chance I got.

We used a lot of rubber mats in the ranch, around the feeders, inside the shelters and so on. We had a big stack of them, about eighteen inches high, stored just outside the wall of the indoor, waiting to be dispensed at a later time.

I decided it would be great idea to have Lyric climb up on the pile.

Lyric climbed the stack of rubber mats without hesitation having once again regained her trust in me. We stood and paused on the pile for few seconds, when I asked her to step down, the mat slid and moved slightly backward under feet. This bothered her and she left the pile in a bit of a huff.

Not having quite learned my lesson, I decided that we hadn't left the mat on a "good note" and we needed to do it again, immediately, and step off more calmly. This time Lyric was much more hesitant to get on. I insisted. She complied only to leave the mat even faster which in turn made the mat move even more under her feet, scaring her further.

So what did I do? I started obsessing over this situation. I had to get her confident with these mats. Why? Who the hell knows!? The more I tried, the worse things got and very quickly, over that one stupid pile of mats, I once again betrayed my sacred oath and main objective of keeping her safe and gave priority to the task getting done instead.

I lost Lyric again. She rightfully and quickly reverted to being a nervous, untrusting and insecure horse.

If only I had a time machine!

But we've already established that I don't.

So it was back to not square one, but minus one hundred!

We went back to ground work again and some easy stuff. Just spending time, taking her with me to do various chores and not asking for anything.

A few more months went by and we were in the indoor exercising and stretching her legs a bit. She looked calm and solid again.

Some of you reading this may be yelling at me "Don't do it!!! Not again!!!"

I did.

I hopped on her bare back and moved around a little. She felt amazing. I saw the garrocha pole leaning against the fence. I sidled her up to it and picked it up, really carefully and slowly. She was fine. "Okay, nothing fancy," I promised as we just carried it and went back to the fence. "See? Just like I promised," I said to her. I laid the garrocha pole back against the fence vertically, but as luck would have it, it slipped, hitting each rail on the way down making some pretty good noise and landed right between Lyric's legs. Her hind feet touched it and she kicked it forward which hit the back of her front feet scaring the crap out of her, kicking it back towards the hind again and before you know it, she was frantically kicking this pole back and forth stuck between her front and hind. It ping ponged like that for a few times before she lost her mind and took off bucking, dumping me in the process.

Three times a charm?

Maybe *she* had finally learned her lesson to not ever trust me again!

I wouldn't have trusted me again after the first one!

But she did.

A fourth time.

After a few months of giving her a break from me, Lyric agreed to give me a fourth shot. I had learned my lessons, but things would never be the same again. She had forgiven me but never forgotten. I had doubt whether the trust and confidence she had in me would ever be restored.

Lyric agreed to work with me again but there was a limit of sticking to the basics. Halter, groom, tack and ride three gaits and occasionally assist me in moving some horses around, that's it. I never tried anything beyond that with her. Things had an outward appearance of being fine, but they didn't feel right. I kept telling Christa something was wrong. Something was lost. So she agreed to take Lyric over and work with her for an additional month. Once Christa was satisfied that Lyric felt solid with the basics, a friend of ours who had fallen in love with her bought her. The good news was that she kept boarding Lyric at our place and life improved for her drastically with a new person who didn't get her in trouble. Her faith in people began restoring. Lyric stayed with us until a few years later when we decided to sell the Aldergrove ranch and move to Pritchard. At that point our friend had to move Lyric out to another barn. As destiny would have it, half a year after that Lyric back came to us again at the Pritchard location, since our friend had just had a baby and wasn't able to spend much time with her.

Lyric happily joined her old friends and some new ones at the new location running on a quarter section with the herd. Of course she needed to get her feet trimmed which meant she had to deal with me again. I did just the bare minimum of ground work with her, enough to have her stand still for getting her feet trimmed. She felt pretty hot and worked up but I managed to relax her with minimal support, just playing on line in the field and quietly moving her quarters around for a few seconds and leaving it.

A few months later when the new barn was finally built, I brought her up and she was acting quite bothered and insecure (primarily due to being taken away from the herd) in the new space with tie stalls at the open end of the barn. The old me would have gotten proactive about it. The new me didn't do anything. I didn't care for playing the trainer and treating her discomfort as a challenge. I just groomed her, picked her feet and put her back out.

I haltered her a week later and brought her back to the same spot. She was a different horse. Totally relaxed, and at ease with the tie stall. I looked at her and smiled and said, "Hey I think I'm finally starting to get it."

She just looked at me and raised an eyebrow.

I'm not sure if "doing nothing" is an accurate account of what happened or, should I say, what didn't happen.

Lyric was pretty amped up and I responded accordingly by adjusting my energy, the tone of my asks and more importantly the time intervals, the spaces of nothings between the asks, taking me all the way back to the lessons learned from Fire on a much deeper and finer level. One of the most important things this did for Lyric was it sent a loud and clear message that I had acknowledged how she was feeling. She knew this by the adjustments I made in my tone and body language in accordance to her energy and state of mind expressed through her body. She felt heard and, more importantly, realized that I cared about her feelings. This was a big change for us in contrast to our previous history of interactions.

Just watching us, you would have only seen a guy grooming a horse, but during this simple task there was a lot of two-way communication going on between us. I would ask her to move her hind feet just a fraction of an inch at a time. I would ask to brush her forelock and wait for her okay before proceeding. Tiny little spaces and pauses between the actions that were responsible for giving meaning and semantics to a language between the two bodies engaged in a physical conversation in complete silence. The spaces and pauses that determined and gave shape to the new relationship between us. The spaces that were missing in our previous interactions a few years back.

Lesson Learned

Sometimes a horse gets so amped up that there is no space for me to ask for anything.

Recently, I was able to employ the lessons learned from Lyric when I was working with a very explosive, troubled mare.

The mare had lost a lot of confidence through some mishaps with her owner, somewhat similar to what Lyric had gone through with me.

On a particular day I was working with her, and as soon as I got on I could feel her under me like a volcano that was about to burst. I had gotten on the day before and cantered with her and she was fine. But that was that day, and this day she was a different horse. So I waited before asking for anything. It didn't matter, she wasn't calming down and was getting more amped by the second. Carefully, I got off as I felt there was no room for me to ask for anything at all. The old me wouldn't have. The old me would have been trying to squeeze more out of her in a damaging pursuit of what I used to consider "a good note to leave on." But not this time; I knew to put her away. After lessons learned from Lyric, to me this was now the new definition of "leaving on a good note." I recognized she had already given me everything she could muster, and there was no point in asking for more at that moment.

The next day I got on and she gave me all three gaits again.

The day after that I got on and she felt explosive again.

So I waited again.

And this time she did calm herself down. She made space for me where there was no space before, and that was our major breakthrough.

So, many thanks to Lyric for the lessons that took me years to digest, which makes me wonder, if I did have a time machine would I go back and change anything?

If it's at the expense of omitting these lessons, then no. I wouldn't change a thing.

3 LEADERSHIP QUALIFICATIONS

Ginger

Fire the stallion was a gentle teacher. Not so much my mare Ginger . . . the stallion! I usually think of mares as female stallions, unadulterated and fully intact.

She was my first horse. Christa insisted that this two-year-old rescue mare was my destiny and I had to get her. She saddle-broke her at three, but I was the first to back her. With not a whole lot of training Christa handed her back to me and said "Good luck!" She was a handful, she told me, and had more spunk than the average horse.

A hot, red-headed half-Appaloosa, half-Arabian mare from hell, Ginger very quickly became and remains to be the love of my life. This mare has more fight in her than flight. She is always at the top of the herd as a trusted leader who is not afraid to kick some serious ass if necessary. Ginger sets the bar very high and you had to be bringing something quite special and impressive to the table if you were going to assume the position of someone who was going to take charge over the space she was in.

Ginger was quite critical and brutally honest. A straight shooter!

In the early days, I remember sitting on the fence of her paddock hanging out and she'd come over and push into my legs dangling off the fence. It was cute and seemingly harmless, but unbeknownst to me at the time, it came with a very important message of space ownership. It was all hers. As long as I yielded and didn't challenge her for ownership, Ginger would allow me to feed her, clean up after her and groom her. But when it came time to put a halter on her and lead her around, things got a little bit complicated.

Ginger did not recognize me as a confident leader. Not to her high standards. I may have been confident enough for the majority of other horses I handled, but not for her.

To use a martial arts analogy, I was qualified for the job of leading white, yellow and orange belts around with my green belt status, but not Ginger. She was a hard core black belt and way above me.

I found her extremely hard to handle on the ground. She knew how to scare me and she did it well. Pushing, shoving me into walls and fences. Throwing me off balance and shaking my foundation. Once, while I was leading her around the property, she ran past me and kicked me in the upper thigh randomly as she went by. Things were no different in the saddle. She had this wonderful judo move she would do if I asked for something she thought I shouldn't have, by slamming on the brakes and dropping her left shoulder down, throwing me to the ground over and over again. It was either that or her other signature move, rearing. But she would never bolt. Every time she threw me off, she'd stand there and wait for me as I scrambled on the ground, putting myself back together and getting back in the saddle.

It was quite discouraging. She would strip me of my confidence and inaccurate self-image on a daily basis. I grew more and more depressed by the day as Ginger would remind that I wasn't qualified to be her horse person.

Frustrated and broken, one day I decided to just turn her loose in the arena to exercise her.

I didn't want to lead her.

I didn't want to ride her.

I was tired of failing with no progress.

So this was the easy way out. Just turn her out. Sit on the fence and wait for her to run around arena for 20 minutes and that's good enough for the day, I thought to myself.

But alas, Ginger would not have this coward's way out.

She started picking up speed with each lap she made around the arena, whizzing past me as I sat on the fence. Each time with a little more gusto, a little more aggression than the last.

She kept getting closer and closer. Pushing into me. Making me pull my head back to avoid getting smacked, trying to get me off the offense.

She was forcing the issue. "You can't stay on the fence. It's this side or that side. Make up your mind!"

I remained on the fence.

So she decided to kick it up a notch, literally, by kicking out at my direction every time she went by.

She wanted to hurt me, I thought.

"She wants to kill me!"

Fed up with flinching, with feeling scared, with feeling humiliated, in a moment of complete insanity, I did the unthinkable as she came galloping towards me. I jumped off the fence, right down on her path and said, "You wanna kill me??? Do it!!! Just run me down and get it over with!"

It was a very Hollywood moment, I admit, but I wasn't bluffing, I had really had enough.

To my extreme shock and relief, Ginger slammed on the brakes and came to a sliding halt four feet from where I had claimed my space and stood my ground.

She stood there with a sweet look on her face, ears forward, eyes blinking with those adorable long lashes, and settled into a neutral stance.

Finally, I had faced the fears that held me back from qualifying as a leader. Someone worthy of taking the lead line and protecting her from danger.

Your horse will never fully trust you to take care of them if they know you are scared or intimidated by them.

Later I would learn that this extreme measure and stupidity are not necessary in expressing courage. There are much safer ways of showing your horse you're not scared. A runaway horse or truly scared horse would have run me down without even knowing it. I can't explain exactly what happened with Ginger except that she, like Fire, was hell bent on teaching me a very important lesson and provided me with a key tool I needed to do my job better and up my qualifications.

Ginger and I messing with the garrocha pole

Pushing cows

Ginger and I hanging out

Fear Management

Along the way there were many other horses who helped me develop courage and fear management when it comes to handling difficult and dangerous situations. Many of them were off the track Standardbreds that had developed some major extreme reactions to the simplest requests.

Years ago I volunteered at a horse rescue that specialized in re-homing these ex-track Standardbreds. These horses took great offense to being asked to perform a circle to the right on line. They also reacted strongly to being asked to move the shoulders, that would sometimes result in the horse rearing over my head and striking. Either that or swinging their hind into me with the head turning to the outside and bolting. Quite dangerous and scary.

A Standardbred taking great offense to moving shoulders laterally

Fear is an interesting topic to me. Throughout the years of working many problem horses I've realized that a lack of fear can get you killed. Without it you can blindly and ignorantly put yourself in situations that could cost you your life. Ego is one of the major contributing factors in getting us in trouble, but fear can keep your ego in check.

I remember when I was a teenager I got a job at a butcher's shop and they had me working the band-saw. One wrong move and the fingers would have come off. This thought horrified me to no end as a guitar player. I told my boss about my fears and he said something very interesting to me. "As long as you have that fear and respect at the back of your mind, you will be alright. The day you get cocky and comfortable with the saw, is the day you lose your fingers," he said as he held up some incomplete digits to my face.

Being around a lot of horses I have learned never to take horse power for granted and have developed healthy respect for the strength and power they hold. But fear must be managed and kept under control in order to be useful.

Cactus Jack

A client of ours had recently purchased a property. The previous owners had taken all their horses with them except for one. Cactus Jack. We figured he was about 12 years or so and must have had some Morgan in him. He was thick and muscular, about 15.2 hands and approximately 1100 lb. It became clear to our client pretty quickly why the previous owners had left him behind. He was aggressive and a bully and had managed to break some of her fingers during some basic ground work sessions. She'd sent him off to a few trainers with no significant change in his behaviour and attitude.

Wanting to try to test what I had learned from my shit picker lessons, I begged and pleaded to work with him for just the cost of hay.

I had been horsing around with our own horses and even started one of the young Arabs bred at home, but I had never taken on an outside "training project." The pressure was on and I had no idea what to do. Where to start. So I decided a good place to gauge things was to take him for a walk around the property the first day he was dropped off at our place.

Cactus was pushy and rushing. And the further we got from the paddocks the more anxious he grew. I was leading him by the shoulder and he was controlling the speed. The faster the pace got, the more nervous I grew. Or was it the other way around? It was all escalating quite rapidly and he finally decided he was going to leave me behind and take off. Of course, being inexperienced, I was determined to hang on to the lead line for as long as I could, instead of as long as I should. It was a 12 foot line which put me directly behind his hind legs as he took off ahead of me. I lost my footing and went down, dragging behind him for a good length before I gave up and finally let go of the rope and watched him take off through the dust he had kicked up at my face.

I got up and dusted myself off, knowing I had bitten off far more than I could chew. I was coughing and choking. So, reluctant and terrified, I started searching for him.

Eventually, I was able to catch up with Cactus at the mares' field where I found him flirting and showing off his muscles over the fence to a captive audience of very interested and impressed mares. To me it looked like he was telling them what he'd just done and they were all laughing at me. Nervous and shaking, humiliated and defeated, I picked up his lead line lying in the dirt and bee-lined him back to his paddock, praying the whole time that he wouldn't take off on me again.

I was scared, but not as scared as I was the next day looking out the window at him in his paddock, trying to build up the courage to go out there and continue "training" him.

I couldn't muster the courage. I was overwhelmed and had no idea what to do. "This is ridiculous," I thought to myself. "I can't stay in the house all day. I should at least put on my boots and step outside. I know I can do that." So I did. Then I convinced myself to pick up the halter just to carry, with no intentions of haltering him, and just walk up to his paddock to look at him. So I did. Then I thought, "Well, why don't I just step into his paddock and move him around a little bit. I know I can do that." So I did. Before I knew it, I had a halter on him and I was bringing him to the barn for a grooming. Slowly, step by step I was learning how to conquer and control my fears.

The fear and respect I had for Cactus never went away, I just learned to manage it, one step at a time. One breath at a time.

Every day Cactus and I would build on what we had felt confident in doing the previous day, and before long we managed to get through a whole lot together. Eventually the grooming led to the round pen for ground work which later led to tacking and backing, and within a few weeks we were enjoying a functional, trusting arrangement that never really lost sight of or respect for horse power, but was not governed or limited by it.

Cactus taught me fear management which allowed me to think my way through the challenges he presented me. You can't think if the fear takes you over. You can't think when you're mad, which is one of the most common side-effects, escalations and expressions of fear.

You don't get rid of the fear, you rise above it, let it guide you into good decisions. Control it, so you can put yourself into a problem solving state of mind, stay calm and think your way through, while being fully aware of the dangers and potentially fatal consequences you face.

These are skills that we see well developed in first responders, especially fire fighters and medics.

Once I was in a thinking mode, things became quite fun with Cactus.

One of the main issues Cactus had was pulling while tied. He was very methodical about it. He would first gently test the lead line to see if it was tied solid by putting a bit of pressure on it. Once he was convinced it was tied solid, he would rock his weight to the hind and break whatever the lead line was tied to. It was a noisy, dangerous, destructive and intimidating exhibition of his power. After he had broken the tie, he would casually stand there looking quite accomplished and pleased with himself, as if to say, "Tada! Look what I can do!!!"

Once I got over being startled and intimidated by this routine I was able to put my thinking cap on, experiment and look for solutions to this misbehaviour.

I brought him into the tie stall as usual but only pretended to tie him and kept the lead line firmly in my hand. He tested it gently to see if it was tied solid by taking the slack out of the line and was convinced that it was. As soon as he rocked his weight to the hind to break the line with all his might, I let go of the rope and he fell on his ass, losing his footing, completely shocked. It was like pulling a chair out from under him.

He never pulled again.

There was a big lesson to be learned here.

Cactus avoiding brace, photo by W.Pugsley

He was looking for something to brace against, and the second he'd find it, he would push or pull against it until it gave. Same thing in the saddle. I'd pick up the reins and as soon as he could feel me, he'd start pulling or pushing through with some serious horse power. I wondered, what if I were to pick up the reins so he could feel me and the second he went to pull, I disappeared so he had nothing to brace against, pushing and pulling against air, and reappeared and became present again the second after he'd failed to brace against something?

I tried it and it worked.

It's very important to not confuse this with a release. The release is there to show and reward the horse that they have found the right answer. This was altogether a different thing. Cactus relied on having something to brace against to exert his power and dominance. He was looking for it like someone looking for a fight. Once he felt it was there in the reins, he would use it to plow into. But like in the tie stall, every time he thought he'd found something solid and committed to plowing through, I'd take it away, like pulling the chair from underneath him. He would lose his balance and feel compromised, only to find me again a split second later with light contact, offering help.

It worked.

But did I trick him or did he just teach me how to handle my reins and lead line?

I don't know, maybe a bit of both?

Either way, Cactus went on to becoming a successful trail horse when he went home.

This was an incredible success for me being a total a novice, and with it came a lot of unfounded self-confidence which would later come back and bite me in the ass. But we'll get to that.

Reading Intentions

The Worming Experiment

I always say "Never play poker with a horse"!

A horse's ability to accurately interpret body language and determine true intention is one of the main reasons they've been so successful at survival for so long.

They know if you're scared. They know if you're mad. They know it when you're happy and when you're sad. All through body language and posture that speak so much louder and always truer than words.

But more importantly they know your intentions. They know if you come in peace or with something else on your mind.

Just recently, at the current ranch location in Pritchard, I watched one of our horses, with the entire herd behind him, slowly and carefully approach a lone coyote. They stood still   and stared at each other for about five minutes. They then closed the gap and touched noses!!

I couldn't believe my eyes.

After the touch, the lone coyote turned around and trotted away. A few moments after watching the coyote leave, the entire herd went back to grazing, no longer at attention. It was one most amazing things I have witnessed to date.

There was a profound exchange of information, intention and treaty. And it looked like they shook hands on it by touching noses.

I can only guess what it may have been.

The horses interact with many other animals on the acreage, birds, deer, coyotes, elks and the occasional passing bear.

The coyotes and the birds feast on the field mice. It looked to me as if the coyote was declaring they meant no harm, and were happy to share the land.

Only the horses and coyotes know for sure.

The deer, on the other hand, were not welcomed at all by the horses. After a short few months of sharing the acreage with them, the horses chased the deer out pretty aggressively, off the land and over the fence. Again, I can only assume it's because the horses realized they didn't care to share their grass with them.

In this bizarre twist of events, it was the herbivores that posed a threat to the horses' interests, not these particular carnivores! I'm sure there wouldn't be much of a conversation at all if it were cougars we were talking about. Cougars would need a little more than just field mice to satisfy them.

Years back, in trying to learn how precise horses are at reading our intentions, I decided to run a little experiment.

We had a field with four geldings in it who all needed worming. One of the barn girls and I were discussing the very topic of horse intelligence and how skilled they are at reading intentions, when we came up with a fun idea to try. We decided, instead of heading out there to worm all four, we would pick just two. We chose to worm Oliver, the wise old Arabian school horse, and Cisco, the imbalanced, damaged-goods Kiger mustang, leaving the other two alone for the time being.

All four geldings were busy with their heads down at their hay piles when we drove up. We parked the gator a few feet ahead of the gate and by the time we stepped out, the two, Oli and Cisco, lifted their heads and walked away from their hay piles to avoid us while the other two completely ignored us and continued to eat.

We were amazed.

You can't sneak up on them.

You can't hide your intentions.

It was a clear message and lesson.

So then the onus falls on us to make our intentions something acceptable and pleasant for the horses to consider when we're approaching them if we don't want them running off when they see us coming.

It brought up an interesting challenge though. What if your horse doesn't want what you have to offer but it's necessary for them to have it regardless?

Say for example, a horse who might have an infection and you must give him his antibiotics daily to address it.

Fire once had such an infection and was prescribed antibiotics. If you recall from earlier, he lived in a three acre field with three geldings. The first couple of oral administrations of antibiotics went okay, but after that he was determined he really didn't care for it, as I suspect he found the taste quite objectionable. The easy solution would have been to bring him into a stall and medicate him there. He would be much easier to catch and halter there. But we wanted to avoid stalling him if possible. As none of the horses at the Aldergrove ranch was stabled, he would have had quite an unpleasant week of solitude for the duration of his medication period. So the hard way it was, catching a horse who knew what was up and did not want to get caught in a three acre field.

There was no sneaking up on him. There was no hiding my intentions. Even if I managed to trick him today, there's no way he'd fall for the same trick tomorrow.

I had to catch my horse, before haltering my horse.

He had to be convinced to be caught at liberty, so he'd just stop running and stand still to be haltered.

But how??

The task was done through an understanding of what I call the point of engagement.

The Point of Engagement

I don't like using mechanical analogies for horses. Horses are much more than that, but they are also that. We all are. Our biomechanics under certain circumstances and context can be compared to vehicular mechanics.

If you know how to drive a standard, this analogy will come easy to you. If not, hang in there and hopefully it will become clear.

The point of engagement when using your clutch is the point at which the clutch starts to engage the power of the engine to the gear box, creating or causing movement in the vehicle.

Through my times spent with horses, I started paying attention and wondering at what point does the movement of my body create movement in my horse or anybody else for that matter?

Different horses have different points of engagement similar to the clutch systems on different vehicles. But horses as we know are obviously much more than mechanical objects, so the point of engagement does not just vary from horse to horse, but can also change for the same horse depending on circumstances such as space itself, energy, intention, emotional state of mind, external stimulations and relational dynamics of the body or bodies present in that space.

Think of how our bodies move and adjust when someone enters or leaves a space we are in. The moment your body commits to physically move and adjust itself, motivated by the presence or absence of another body, is what I'm calling the point of engagement. Imagine how you might move if you're on a bus as it becomes more or less crowded. Imagine how your body would move or position itself if you were sharing that space with someone drunk or hostile as opposed to calm and sober. All of these variables will influence and determine your "point of engagement" and the manner in which it engages.

Ironically I used the very lessons Fire had taught me about the mechanics of moving his body using mine to catch him and medicate him against his wishes.

My intentions were obviously not to harm him, quite the opposite. I was fulfilling my duties as a caregiver by giving him his medication and promoting his health and wellness. I know he knew that, otherwise I would have never been able to catch him. He knew I meant well but still didn't care for the disgusting taste of the antibiotics.

Fire's point of engagement had become hypersensitive due to the fact that he did not want what I was offering. My approach would send him running to quite a distance at the mere sight of me, of course, but only when I was carrying the medication (which also happened at a set time of the day). So he knew very well what was coming and what I was up to.

His point of engagement during this process was set at a range of about 50 to 100 feet. That meant he would start moving and reacting to my body when I was within this range.

But the longer the distance, the easier my job got.

Sounds odd doesn't it?

This is how it worked. With the point of engagement set at such a long range, I was able to access Fire's drive lines with the slightest change of angle in my body from a distance away.

That meant I was able to influence his direction, get ahead of him, stop him and send him in the opposite way as if by remote control despite the fact that he was keeping his distance.

Fire would attempt to run from the direction of the pressure only to find me ahead of him with a slight turn of my shoulder and mid-section, still connected to his drive line at a distance. A few attempts at outrunning the pressure and he'd stop, yield and stand still while I approached and haltered him. I could tell by observing his body change from active to a neutral stance, grounded with muscles relaxed at rest, which usually comes with the feet fairly squared up, the balance centred, and eyes and ears on me.

It wouldn't always go that smoothly and sometimes he'd take off when I was much closer and more easily deked out. But that's where Fire was teaching me patience. I would just set it up and try again and again until I got it right. If I got it right, I would notice the task becoming easier at every attempt instead of harder.

Whatever I'm doing with my horse, I always try to remember to ask myself, "Is it getting better or worse? Is it getting harder or easier? Is it getting uglier or prettier?" as means of policing myself and gauging my work and its effects on my horse.

I had to learn to keep my emotions in check and not let anger take over through frustration, because there's literally nothing attractive about angry energy and I would just end up repelling my horse further and farther away from me.

The concept of the point of engagement became extremely helpful to me when doing ground work or in the saddle. It made me pay attention and become aware of the point at which my horse would start to move and respond to an aid or ask, which in turn helped me determine the point at which "release" should happen.

The point of engagement is one of those universal laws that applies to everything, living or not. Try it with birds, cats, dogs, people to see at what point your body causes movement in theirs.

This is not just useful with living beings, it's helpful with non-sentient objects as well. With my students, one of the things we enjoy doing is finding the point of engagement in our bits and halters. For example, one student can hang the halter off the back of their hands with their eyes closed while the other picks up the lead line and starts moving it. The student with closed eyes determines the point of engagement as soon as she starts feeling and receiving the slightest movement and signal from the nose band in the halter.

It sounds silly, but you'd be surprised how different the point of engagement can be in each halter, depending on the design, material and weight of not just the halter but also the lead line attached to it. The build and material used in our tack significantly determine its quality as a conduit for signal. Cheap ropes with no core and poorly designed or made halters are terrible conduits and dead to the feel. This hinders the halter as an effective means of communication with the horse, leaving us relying on other means to communicate in compensation. Knowing this will change how you might handle your horse depending on what kind of halter is available to you at the time. There's a world of difference between a web halter and rope halter in functionality. With most web halters the signal is significantly deadened where the line clips to the ring. In contrast, with most rope halters the signal is carried from the rope through to the halter, again depending on the stiffness and thickness of the rope halter itself. There can be a world of difference between one rope halter and another.

The same can be done with different bits, holding the bit between two hands clasped together, with another student manipulating the reins. At what point do you feel the bit move? At what point does the bit engage?

This sort of experimenting can also help us determine the amount of pressure necessary to instigate movement, and more importantly helps us get a rough idea of what our horses are experiencing through different tack. Having access to this information can drastically change the way we use our equipment and help us adjust our approach in an educated manner.

It also helps get a sense between physical pressure and signal.

By employing an understanding of point of engagement, learned from Fire himself, I was able catch him and medicate him twice daily for ten days in the three acre field. But we've only talked about half the equation here.

Engaged versus Evasive Movement

The space was already defined by the perimeter fencing. The ownership of space was already given and established. The problem now was that Fire simply did not want to share my space as long as I had the medication with me due to his aversion for the oral dose of antibiotics.

This is where I needed to utilize yet another lesson learned from Fire and other horses about the difference between what I call an **engaged** versus **evasive** response. My usage of the term "engaged" here is to describe the relationship between two bodies, but not in the usual muscular context.

I will use the round pen setting to try to explain what I mean by an engaged movement as opposed to an evasive one.

When moving a horse in a round pen I always ask myself, "Where would the horse be if it weren't for the panels in the pen?" I've applied pressure and the horse has been convinced to move away. If the nature of this movement is an evasive one, then without the round pen panels keeping the horse in the space, the horse would be gone. But if I have managed to win the trust of the horse and his acceptance of me as a qualified safe leader, while still moving, the horse would not take off into space like a comet shooting out of the orbit but would instead emulate a satellite, a moon if you will, that orbits around me, bound by a voluntary and chosen magnetic or gravitational pull. That's what I mean by engaged in this context.

To truly test this gravitational pull, I often use larger pens or riding arenas to verify the existence of such a phenomenon, but it can easily be demonstrated in a round pen as well.

Creating a gravitational pull on horseback

If and when the gravitational pull is established or created, you will be able to influence the size of the circles the horse is using to orbit around you from small to large and vice versa. You will be able to create not just a push outward but also a pull inward.

By that I mean one can create a space by drawing back and have the horse fill that space respectively as if drawn into a vacuum.

This is what Fire was initially teaching me about that day when he was moving his body in relation to my body movements. If I tilted my balance in, he would withdraw and if I pulled back, he would fill in the now available space. A gentle see-saw of shifting and yielding our centres of balance in relation to one another.

It literally becomes a dance.

It's been nearly 15 years since Fire taught me that tutorial and to this day I'm still reflecting and discovering new depths to the profundity of what he was showing me.

It's humbling and mind boggling as I feel like I'm still barely touching the tip of a massive and monumental iceberg of knowledge that I just can't imagine being able to fully explore in just one lifetime.

But I digress, again . . .

Back to the field with Fire, now standing at a neutral stance. As I closed in with the medication I had to pay careful attention to Fire's centre of balance. If I approached too fast, without his consent, surpassing his comfort zone, he'd be gone and I would have to start from scratch. So how did I determine where to stop?

Well at first it was mainly through trial and error. I knew I had gone past his comfort zone when he'd leave. Pretty obvious. But there were plenty of clues I learned to pick up on before he committed to flight. As I mentioned before and probably will again a thousand times, I had to keep a keen eye on his centre of balance. He would shift his weight in preparation of moving before he moved his legs, and before that, if my eyes were keen enough, I would notice an isometric change in his muscles and an overall tension in his body.

I had to catch myself, stop and wait at the point before he committed to movement. Drop all pressure and make sure my body was at a neutral centre of balance, so the horse would not be pushed or pressured and would stand still. The next step was to wait. Wait until I saw a change in my horse, back to neutral. I found that a smart move at the edge of the point of engagement was to draw back, creating a vacuum or negative space. The horse would most of the time fill the space in by a turning an ear, an eye and maybe even a full head in my direction. This was a huge and significant change I had made possible for my horse, not only in the direction he would move physically, but also by causing a psychological shift to becoming a willing participant who had a negotiating voice in the matter.

Let's use the vehicle analogy again to help grasp this idea a little bit better. If my car is in drive and I push down on the gas pedal, the car is going to move forwards. If I have it in reverse, pressing the gas pedal is going to drive the car back. The position of the wheels will further determine the direction of the forward or backward movement the vehicle will take (left or right).

If you relate this analogy to horses, pressure is the accelerator, the direction is expressed by the balance of the horse and where he's looking. If my horse is already in forward mode, any pressure applied is going to result in a forward movement towards the direction his balance and head are pointing. In this particular situation, I need to make sure I'm not applying pressure to the horse when he is geared up to move forward and away. By creating a vacuum, waiting for the ear, eyes and head to look to the inside, I can influence my horse to change his direction towards me instead of away from me. Any pressure registered now towards the hind of the horse will result in a step towards me instead of away from me.

As you may already know, this can change in a split second by the horse looking back out and away from me again. I have to be quick enough and in control enough of my body to make sure if this happens I am immediately dropping any kind pressure with my body and balance that would cause a forward and unwanted movement from my horse. To some people this may look like you're sneaking up on your horse, but it could not possibly be anything further from that. It may look like you're walking on egg shells around your horse and that, also, is not at all the interaction that is happening here. We are literally engaged in a two way conversation where the horse is choosing which direction they want to travel in relation to the pressure they're registering from the handler. We are asking, negotiating and offering something that the horse may or may not consent to.

Horses in general don't like exerting and wasting a lot of energy if it's not absolutely necessary. Their survival instincts favor conserving energy for when they really need it, running from predators. That doesn't mean they don't go for a run once in a while or horse around with each other. They do. In very short spurts, on their terms.

Fire already knew I was not a predator and not interested in killing and eating him. He knew exactly what I was offering. A horrible tasting medicine. He then had to make a choice and weigh his options, "Do I accept the offer, the invite of coming in at the expense of getting the disgusting meds or do I keep running?" He knew I was persistent and dedicated. He knew I wasn't going anywhere until he had his meds. He knew I meant him no harm. And most importantly, I believe he appreciated that I was asking and waiting for his consent instead of trying to sneak it on him or trick him into taking it by force or restricting his mobility. So, he took a step in and allowed me to halter him and reluctantly took his meds.

I reassured him by letting him know there's only a few more days of this nonsense and that I don't like it any more than he does. I may have vocalized these thoughts out loud to him. Not that it was necessary. I had no illusions about him understanding English, but I knew he was capable of feeling the sentiment and the energy behind my words. After many years of doing this I have found myself using fewer and fewer words and simply relying on the fact that our intentions are loudly echoed, expressed and crystal clear through our body language that horses read so well. I have come to appreciate a much more subtle, private and invisible-to-the-average-eyes-and-ears version of communicating with my horses.

No it's not psychic, not for me anyways. It's body language, subtle, articulated, crystal clear, and honest. No whispering for me, thanks.

The Player's Game

Simply having a handle on the mechanics of how things work is not enough. Reducing the interaction to the base physical properties of moving bodies can limit us in accessing much greater possibilities and potential for sophisticated and meaningful symbiotic relationships.

I have been to many clinics where I watch simple principles of physics at work. The trainer, using a stick or lunge whip, taps the horse on the shins to cause a stop or a back-up. These methods work. They work very well as they are in accordance with basic physical facts and the horse's natural response and aversion to physical discomfort. The horse feels a physical barrier presented and stops or backs away to avoid the unpleasant tapping. The horse can be taught many things through similar methods such as pulling back on the reins and causing physical discomfort that motivates the horse to seek relief.

To me these methods are no different than exerting pressure behind a car to manually push it off the road. It works. The principles of physics demand it. But something else also works and in complete accordance with the laws of physics and science: getting in the car, turning on the engine and driving it while letting the engine do all the work with minimal physical exertion and pushing and pulling on our part.

You can physically push your horse around using various kinds of tack and tools or you can tap into something much more sophisticated the horse has to offer, equine automation!

All of a sudden you discover you can go from manual steering to power steering! From forcing a movement to inspiring one and with real horse power.

But we can only get access to this kind of horse power and hydraulic luxury through winning our horse's willing cooperation in moving as one with us, because ultimately their vessel, their body, belongs to them, as ours belongs to us.

One of my favourite questions to ask students is, "If you were to compare your tack to car parts, which car part would your reins be?"

Almost 100% of the time the answer is steering wheel.

What would you say it is?

If you also said steering wheel, I humbly disagree.

Can you use your reins as a steering wheel? Absolutely. Most people do, and sometimes you might have to in order to avert disaster. But should you? I don't think so, not as a regular mode of function. Just like you wouldn't use the emergency brake in your car as a primary means of slowing down or stopping your car.

In my opinion the reins are better used similarly to how we use our turn signals. On your car, some of you will use your signals to communicate to other commuters which direction you're going. Similarly, on your bridle you can use your reins to communicate with your horse which direction you wish to go. I shouldn't have to turn my horse, I should just be able to ask and let him do it. If I get out of his way and let him do it, he will have the chance to do it right, balanced, with the proper muscle engagement for frame and head position available to him under the specific circumstances and capability. He will do it with confidence and no resistance.

Don't be tricked into thinking of your horse as the car in this analogy. Your horse is the other living, breathing, thinking being we are trying to communicate our directions to.

My body is my vessel and the horse's body is his. All we are trying to do is link our bodies so we can move our vessels in unison and synchronicity. Resorting to pushing, pulling and forcing as the principle means of moving our horse leaves a very important part of the equation behind, the horse's mind and with it his soul.

I think of it as a couple or as a parent and child holding hands, walking together. Pushing, pulling, shoving all of a sudden becomes inappropriate and rude, unless you're saving their lives by getting them to stop from stepping into traffic.

Horses can be trained by force. It works. I just find it limiting when compared to the fantastic possibilities that they can offer as willing and respected partners.

In order for our bodies to connect in this manner, I must try to connect our minds first, all of which happens through using spatial negotiation and understanding.

As I mentioned before with Fire, I had to negotiate not just physically but psychologically in order for him to agree to take his meds.

Sometimes the negotiations are predominantly psychological when it comes to sharing space.

Here's a funny story.

There were a couple of mares who came under our care that were turned out with five other mares in an oval shaped field at the centre of our track that we called, well, The Oval.

These two were joined at the hips. One of them was social and easy to catch, the other would run and take off at a mere glance. I wasn't sure what her story was at the time and I didn't care. She was never in my way and did a good job flying under my radar undetected, which, as far as this shit picker was concerned, was just perfect.

Late one cold evening just when I was about to call it a day and leave the barn, the farrier came in and asked for some help. She couldn't catch the shy one of the duo, Angel, and the owner, who wasn't there, had asked for her to be trimmed. I was still relatively new to this horse care business but always looking for an opportunity to tackle a challenge that might help me get better with horses and give me some credibility with horse people.

Well, here it was.

Catch that mare.

The farrier said she had been out there for a bit and tried various things but the damn mare just would not be haltered. I said "Okay. It's dark, it's starting to snow a bit and neither one of us wants to be out here longer than necessary. Give me ten minutes and if I can't figure something out by then, we'll both go home."

No time for shenanigans, running around, trying to physically catch a horse, that's just stupid and futile. So what to do?

Five minutes later I came back to the barn with the mare who wouldn't be caught.

The farrier, knowing I was relatively new to the horse scene, was tickled and asked, "How did you manage that so fast?"

So I told her, not having a ton of horse experience, I drew on lessons and strategies learned during my days as a bachelor.

"What?" she laughed.

"Well I remembered when I was single and I saw a girl I liked at the bar, I had learned not to approach her directly, but to approach and show interest to her friend instead. It was a total game changer for a couple of reasons. First, I was a lot more confident and casual since her friend wasn't the one I was trying to impress. So immediately I was less desperate as it alleviated much of the pressure. Second, her friend (the one I was really into) even if not at all interested in me, which was usually the case, would wonder why I was paying so much attention to and talking to her friend instead of her and was now actually trying to win my attention for the sake of her own sanity. Once at that point, well, I'd just let her win."

We both had a really good laugh about that. Funny, but it was true. That was the strategy I used to catch that mare.

I knew I could approach her buddy. So why not to start with something you can do, as opposed bee-lining it straight for the unachievable? That was my initial step. I had already learned horses can't be tricked. So my frame of mind and intentions were to just hang out with her buddy. Approach her, pet her, and just spend some time, with no intentions of haltering. I truly didn't intend to. I was okay to just go home after hanging out a little, see what happened, perfectly willing to accept the outcome, whatever it may have been. After petting her buddy for a bit, our hard-to-catch mare started getting curious, so I offered her my hand and waited for her to make the initial touch. She did. I left it at that, withdrew my hand and continued to pet her friend. She came back and I offered my hand again. She touched it. This time I briefly touched back but quickly went back to her friend again. Slowly this progressed until she was willingly allowing me to pet her, rub her and just hang. When the time felt right I offered to halter. She agreed. And that's how that happened. Taking your time to get you faster results is what horses have shown me over and over again.

Without the psychological side of the equation it would have been impossible to use the physical techniques about drive lines, pressure and all that other stuff that was **also** required to get this job done. You need both and more.

You have to be honest, genuine and willing to accept the horse's answer to your ask. If my horse is not comfortable with something then I try to find out what it is they are comfortable with and start with that. It may or may not progress past that and that's fine. It usually does, or I'd be out of business.

You can't halter a horse that doesn't want to be haltered short of trapping and physically restraining him, which may be necessary depending on extraneous circumstances, but not acceptable as an everyday routine and ritual. It's just not feasible. If the horse doesn't want to be haltered, something is wrong. Something needs to change. We need to think hard about why.

Being with a handler and interacting should not be something a horse dreads or avoids; it should be something they look forward to, something they enjoy.

So it's time for some serious self-reflection and investigative analysis as to why this horse is dreading being caught or with us. It could be an indication of physical discomfort associated with the work and activities they anticipate. Might be the tack, might be the bit or the way you handle it, might be feeling insecure or compromised during handling or having a distaste for the particular discipline or sport you are engaged in, could be soreness in feet, or back. It could be the stressful or frustrated energy the handler might be putting out. It could be something in their past that had nothing to do with you. Let your horse tell you. Watch them carefully, learn to read their thoughts through their facial and body expressions.

There are a number of studies out there dedicated to reading and interpreting the ever-so-expressive faces of horses. We must do our homework, commit ourselves to the facts and stop making up shit with wishful assumptions, unfounded theories and fairy tales.

At our current location we have all the horses loose on a quarter section. Not only do we need our horses to not run away or avoid us at the prospect of being haltered, but we want them to actually run towards us when they see us coming literally a mile away, competing for our attention and happy to share space. Without this kind of relationship it would be logistically impossible for us to do our jobs of maintaining and caring for them.

We have had many "hard to catch" horses come and stay with us only to change and become willing and enthusiastic or at least tolerant of being haltered in a relatively short amount of time in large open fields.

In all the years and horses I have worked with there was only ever one hard to catch horse that just would not be caught consistently no matter what I tried.

Rain on My Parade

This particular mare was named Rain. A roan quarter horse/Percheron I first met at a ranch in Alberta. She was a little evasive about being haltered, but it didn't take a lot. She had recently joined the trail horse string at this ranch that was geared towards younger kids, some of whom had next to no experience but would visit the ranch for their summer camp, and Rain was proving to be not quite the right fit for the job.

They figured she might be happier in a different setting and Christa, who wrangled there during summers, had fallen in love with her. I was reluctant to add yet another horse to our herd at home, so being the clever lady she is, she had me ride the mare at the ranch in Alberta.

Riding Rain

It was love at first stride. We went on a four hour ride in open country. I tested her on everything I could think of, and she was amazing. So it was a no brainer. Bring her home. She was worth her weight in gold as far as I could tell.

Rain and I chilling at Red Deer River in Alberta

I wasn't too involved with her after that. The mare and Christa were doing great, making leaps and bounds in progress. I do remember getting on her one day, after about a year of being at our place, and noticing she was not reacting well to me in the saddle. She felt nervous, evasive and explosive, none of which was there when she was with Christa, who has a much calmer and more supportive energy than I do. I didn't think anything of it. A few months later Rain and Christa got into a pretty bad wreck when they went with some friends on a four day trip filled with all kinds of fun cowgirl activities, riding and shooting and other fun stuff. They had been doing fantastically until the very last day when they went out for an early morning long trot with other riders.

I wasn't there but I saw the aftermath. Apparently there was a disagreement between Christa and Rain over the pace and speed during the long trot that resulted in Rain bucking and head-butting Christa three times with the back of her head, pulling her hand into the horn of the saddle and breaking it, before Christa came off and Rain took off bucking into the woods. It was brutal with a concussion, broken bones and many hospital visits and eight months of recovery for Christa.

The mare was physically fine but the ordeal had triggered a major set-back psychologically.

Back at home, we needed to figure out what had gone wrong. The first and most obvious problem was that, where she was a little bit shy once in a while about being caught before, she now wouldn't be caught at all anymore. She had also taken to bucking when saddled, where she had never bucked previously, even when she was first started, and had been standing still for saddling for a year! Saddle fit and physical issues were checked out and ruled out.

The sessions would always start out rough but end on a calm and quiet note, only to go back to being rough again the next day. It would take a lot of time and convincing to have her agree to be haltered in the larger field. There were no arguments in the paddock setting, but that's because she knew she was limited in her options in a smaller space. I had to figure out why she didn't want to be caught. I believed this aversion was the underlying key to what went wrong the day of the accident at the ranch. It was clearly something that was triggered by the sight of the halter which meant work. She was very social and people-friendly as long as you did not carry a halter. So we decided to try something out.

Get rid of work.

We put her back in the field with other mares to get an honest reaction about being haltered. After about an hour of negotiating, she finally allowed me to halter her on the first day of my new approach in the field. This was met with plenty of praise and positive feedback from me. I brought her out and took her out to graze on the pasture for half an hour, brought her back and set her loose. No going to the barn, no grooming, no saddling. No work. Just grazing.

The second day it took half the time to halter her. Quite an improvement. The third day she was haltered in less than five minutes. The fourth day she met me at the gate leaving the herd. Same with the fifth day of haltering and grazing. On the sixth day she wouldn't be caught at all. At all!!! After two hours of trying, I gave up. She had worked herself into a sweaty mess running, avoiding being haltered and I had to back off, because it was obvious that she had chosen to run till she dropped and would rather die than let me put a halter on her. That's when I knew I had reached my limit of knowledge and skill. I didn't know what to do for her. I didn't know where to go from there. She was defying logic. Throughout the decades we had worked with many horses who were reluctant to get caught only to have them do a 180 and find confidence and pleasure in spending time with their handler. Not this one.

After consulting with some of our extremely talented horsemen friends and even trying a bucking line as an option for her to no avail or change in behaviour, we ended up sending her back to the original breeders and friends of ours who had started her in Alberta. From what we've heard, she's been doing alright back at home and there have been no major issues.

I will never know for sure what was going on in her head. I wasn't able to figure her out. What I do know is that she was unhappy and not quite functional.

I could have kept her in a paddock and limited her say in the matter, but that wouldn't have gotten me any closer to figuring out why she didn't want to be haltered on her own volition, why she didn't want to connect, why she would shake and act so scared in the barn aisle when I'd try to just touch her, why she wasn't present but somewhere else in mind and spirit. There was no rhyme or reason to it, none that I could see.

There were a lot of "whys" but at the end of the day the main problem was the "whats." Too much time and energy can be wasted, with no practical solution, on "whys" and theorizing. She felt a certain way and

I couldn't figure out "what" to do about it. I have come to realize that knowing the answer to the why a horse might feel a certain way doesn't really change what I need to do about it all that much. If I have a horse that won't tie because they had a traumatic experience once being tied solid, knowing the details of the story won't change what I need to do, the steps I need to take to help that horse feel more comfortable with being tied. The only thing it does, is it helps me empathize with the horse as to why he is behaving that way. Which begs the question, if there was no story, should I then not feel any empathy for the horse that won't tie?

Why is this horse scared of a plastic bag when another is not? Why is this horse scared of yellow boots and the other isn't? It doesn't matter. She just is.

I just need to figure out *what* to do to make her feel better and help her through it.

In some way, asking why can even undermine the legitimacy of the feeling the horse is experiencing. Maybe it's none of my business.

If a horse finds something unacceptable, I don't want to ask her "Why?" I want to ask her "What is acceptable?"

Just because I couldn't figure out what to do to make her feel better doesn't mean there wasn't something there - far from it. The most likely and logical explanation is, I missed something. Whatever it was, given the fact that I didn't have the skills to figure it out, I feel we made the right decision by sending her back to where she seems to be having a better and relatively more functional life.

Purpose

Taking care of a large herd of horses in addition to taking on training projects takes up more time and hours than there are in a day. So, out of sheer necessity, I had to combine the two in some ways to manage all the work I had taken on.

This led to one of the most effective and productive tools in my tool box.

Including my training projects as partners in getting some of my chores done turned out to be one of the most beneficial practices I've stumbled on, so much so that it even influenced and drastically changed the way I work with horses in a round pen/training setting.

The horses were spread out through the Aldergrove property in various fields and paddocks. They all needed the waters checked and topped. Feeders needed to be checked and inspected as horses would often break them, leaving nails sticking out or torn hay nets that needed mending. The same with fences. Stormy weather usually resulted in fallen trees causing all kinds of damage to fences and shelters.

A lot of times I would take a horse with me to deal with these situations, be it under saddle or just leading and bringing them along.

Horses are curious animals and by nature they love exploring and venturing. This gave them a chance to step out and do something, see things and other horses outside of a "training" setting in a round pen or arena. It also provided an excellent opportunity to prove to my horse that I was able to protect him from other pestering horses when we'd go into their fields to check the feeders by keeping the challengers at bay.

The pressure was off drastically as the focus was no longer laser concentrated on the horse. The focus was shifted to the job at hand that were going to do together. I think this caused a major psychological shift in the horses and their opinion of the time and space shared with me.

I'd like to think of it in terms of the "limelight." We can all relate to stage fright and the anxieties related to becoming the main focus of what is happening. With it may come some psychological pressure and insecurities. I think a lot of that pressure is taken off our horses when we're not "working on" them, but "working with" them "on something else." This is why some trainers employ the use of hoof balls, mechanical flags or live cattle as indirect tools of advancing their horses' education.

Working together

I noticed a major difference in Ginger when we'd be just riding or riding with a purpose and job in mind. For example checking the fence in one field that had damaged horse wire and needed mending. Riding back to the workshop to get the necessary tools and riding back up to the field to fix the broken wire. We were on a mission and Ginger needed to humour me with a lot of different obstacles to make the job possible, which included things like stepping into the work shop with me to get the tools and standing still and out of the way while I worked on the mending the fence. Nothing piques a horse's curiosity more than when you're working on something with tools. They really want to see what you're doing and take great interest in how shit works.

I learned about this in a bit of an extreme situation. A cottonwood tree had gone down in the oval field that housed seven mares. I went in there with a chainsaw to check on things and clean up.

I had to work really hard to get the horses out of my hair! You'd think the sound and the hubbub of the chain saw would have sent them running. And it did for about five seconds and twenty feet, but after that there was no satisfying their curiosity short of touching the damn thing, while it was running, with their noses. Clearly I couldn't allow that to happen and I was annoyed to no end, shooing off these damned mares who could not satisfy their curiosity.

It was a big lesson. I immediately thought of all the times a horse was scared of seeing a saddle or shying away from a tarp, etc. I realized I was going about it the wrong way. If you tap into their curiosity, you can get them to brave anything, even a chainsaw.

I realized at that moment that desensitizing a horse may not be the ideal way to go about things. Piquing their curiosity and interest in our activities and tack is a much more effective way of introducing horses to new, "scary" objects. But the main thrust behind all of this was the "purpose" of "a job" that had to get done. Why are we doing this? What's the point? We need to be able to answer these questions.

So with saddle breaking for example, I encourage their curiosity towards the saddle at first. Allow time and space for them to examine, touch, feel, smell and then ask them to carry it for me as part of the "job" at hand. I have them come with me as I carry it first and then ask them if they would carry it now for a bit since I'm getting tired. It's different way of looking at the whole process. Instead of me doing something to them by saddling, I'm asking them to help me with a job that we can do together. I.e., "Help me carry this thing."

With tarps, I give the horse as much space and freedom of movement as my lead line allows, usually a minimum of twelve feet, and I play with the tarp, folding and unfolding it with no pressure or ask from the horse to do anything, allowing the horse time and space to get curious about what I'm doing with the noisy and strange thing I'm playing with. Almost always, the horse will come to check it out for themselves and explore, and in no time will accept being asked to walk on it, over it, drag it and be draped in it.

Accepting the tarp

Building Confidence

Building confidence in your horse and nurturing their curiosity is not the same as desensitizing your horse. Many clients come to me with the ever so popular request of making their horses "bombproof." I find this terminology troubling. I think it misses the mark and the nature of the horse.

You could "bombproof" a horse through training methods that create "helplessness" in your horse. (There's a fantastic book called *Evidence Based Horsemanship* by Martin Black and Stephen Peters that discusses and explains the concept of learned "helplessness" when it comes to training horses.) Instead, you can pique their curiosity and build up their confidence in themselves so they can handle and be safe around unknown objects and situations. Teach them "fear management" just like they taught me.

To me, nothing is worse than a horse who has stopped communicating and has withdrawn from the conversation. I call it "checking-out" or "going to their happy place." This usually happens when the horse realizes that they have no say or choice in the things we are going to subject them to, that their opinion doesn't matter and, worse yet, we don't want to hear it. The most obvious place for me to check to see if that is what the horse is dealing with is the eyes. The eyes will not follow your movements and they remain fixated, blankly staring off into space. The body becomes statuesque and robotic in movement. The yields become exaggeratedly evasive which some may confuse for being "light" and the line of communication becomes much more cue based than feel oriented. The body stiffens which prevents proper engagement of the correct muscles. Everything becomes rigid and jerky. Some of these horses get so terrified about doing the wrong thing that it sometimes becomes difficult to get them to move out at all. I've seen it a few times in Trainer's Challenge Competitions at horse expos, where the trainer went so out of his way to make sure the horse wouldn't move during the initial tacking process, that they could hardly get their horse to move out at all after that, costing them the competition and completely ruining the horse. But hey, at least they were able to stand on the horse's back and crack a bull whip!

Don't get me wrong. I think being able to stand on your horse and cracking a bull whip is awesome, as long as you didn't get there by shutting your horse down. As long as you got there with your horse fully intact, aware, awake and a confident partner.

We have restarted and rehabbed many horses like this and it takes a very long time for them to become somewhat functional again, if ever. However, horses never forget, they might forgive, but they will never forget. It's a real shame. A shut down horse reacts to people in two basic modes. They are either bracing against you or are in some form of evasive flight mode.

Their say and voice in the matter has been taken away and the communication has been reduced from a two way conversation to a one way ticket to Dictatorship-ville.

Interactions during mucking and feeding can go a long way in providing opportunities to show these horses a different side to people and convincing them to maybe give us another chance. It's easier due to the simple fact that we are interacting and attempting to communicate in a non-work setting and the conversation is not about training and dominating but about turf and space. Slowly one can connect the "non-work" interactions to working ones, but it takes a while. For most of these horses, I find the best rehab is to turn them out on a large acreage with other horses so they can take a break from people for a while, before trying to reconnect with them.

4 THE ZEN OF MUCKING

The Early Days

I have vivid memories of the early days, almost two decades ago, when I had never cleaned a stall before. I had temporarily taken over for Christa who was on bed rest, pregnant at the time with our daughter, and I had no idea what I was doing.

Shit picking grin, photo by Mike Scriven

I had never fed "hangry" horses before or led them from stall to paddock and back as our horses lived way back then. Everything that could have gone wrong, did. Kicked, bitten, run over, dragged, humbled over and over again.

Each time I survived I walked away with more than just my life. I walked away with vital bits of information that would increase my chances of avoiding disaster the next time around.

In Richmond, the first location of our business, on a three acre parcel just off of Steveston Highway, we stalled horses. The stalls were heavily bedded with sawdust. The crap piles were easy to spot. But the urine was somewhat hidden. You had to know where to look. Each horse was different. Each horse had their own quirks and squirts. It was the beginning of using my five senses in ways that some may interpret incorrectly as the sixth sense. You get to know where to look through experience and basic investigative skills. It was the same later at the Aldergrove location, where they lived outside in paddocks and it had snowed all night, covering everything under a deceivingly pristine snowy blanket. However, underneath the blanket was at least 60 lbs of horseshit that needed to be located and mucked out. It's not a sixth sense or some kind of magic - it's learning to use your five senses better, faster, sharper. It's what will keep you alive if you learn to use them properly and efficiently.

It's not just brain intelligence, it is muscle intelligence as well. Muscle memory and the fine tuning of your five senses in conjunction with getting to know each horse and remembering their routines to guide you.

You can do stalls and paddocks all your life and not pay attention, and fail to capitalize on the golden opportunities mucking provides in gaining skills vital to becoming a horseman/woman and understanding horses.

This early period of hard lessons in what seemed insignificant tasks was in fact the "wax on, wax off" part of *Karate Kid*, equine style!

It was during these early stages that the seed had been planted. And it would take many years before I would see any signs of growth or fruition.

But that didn't matter.

What mattered was that everything I needed was contained in the DNA of the seed that had been planted in fresh steaming piles of horseshit, and had the potential to become a giant tree given the right conditions.

It would need time, care and love to nurture it into something useful. Something practical. Something universal that would eventually connect the dots. Something with the promise of putting our minds at ease, setting our souls free by placing us back where we belong, in harmony and synchronicity with all that is, at complete peace and submission to all the beauty and horror that is life.

Anyways, I had to go looking for the pee spots hiding under the sawdust.

But before all that, I had to set up the hay in the paddocks and lead the horses out to them. This was the most horrifying part of the job. They were hungry and anxious to get out and to the hay.

The alternative was to feed them in stalls and clean up while they were in there with me. That idea seemed entirely too dangerous to me. At that time, to me, standing behind a horse was the same as staring down the double barrel of a loaded shot gun. So I would get them out first and then muck.

There was a lot to be learned the hard way, leading hungry anxious horses, for a novice thrown to the lions on his own. At that point and time, leading horses for me meant getting them from A to B without dying. I was not interested in anything other than the task at hand.

You realize quickly that the horses in the back of the line grow exponentially more anxious and worked up waiting their turn. You learn that with each horse leaving the barn, the rest grow noticeably more aggressive and impatient. So now you are forced to use your noggin. What the hell to do? I was in over my head. I was getting dragged, pushed into walls and it was getting dangerous.

To save my life I started paying attention to each horse and strategizing using the information available to me. Take the young ones, tough ones, troubled ones out first, leave the older, calmer ones for last. Simple? Yes. Obvious? Maybe not. It's hard to notice the obvious when you're rattled and scared and feel sorry for yourself.

I figured out to pick the closest paddocks to the barn for the difficult ones, and longer distance paddocks for the easier ones.

Scan and remove foreign objects that were not there yesterday that may spook the horses on your path.

Lead them at their shoulder so when the shit hits the fan you won't get run over.

Two of my teachers were Sammy and Dallas.

Sammy

I recall once I was leading this 16+ hand thoroughbred named Sammy. I was slightly ahead of him as we walked down the barn aisle past a pair of yellow boots. His legs split apart as he came to an abrupt halt. He went from being almost 17 hands high to half the height and I found myself staring, bug eye to bug eye, with a horse that usually towered over me. He'd seen gum boots before. But NOT YELLOW ONES!!!!!!

He snorted with his eyes bulging as I yanked on him to keep him walking with no success. Finally he decided to be brave and forge ahead. The boots were just past his barrel, behind him, when he decided to pick up some extra speed to avoid getting attacked from the rear. Well. He went over me. Clearly, to him, I was the perfect emergency exit to safety with no space ownership. That was the first time I saw the under belly of a horse from the ground up.

I was lucky. He never touched me except for the initial knock down to the ground. He took himself into one of the empty paddocks with hay in it. Good thing I had left the gates to each expecting paddock open. Now I was thinking ahead!!

Dallas

I learned to pay attention to where the horse is in relation to me at all times, the hard way.

I was in a paddock on a sunny day with a little cute filly maybe two years old. I lost sight of her as I mucked. Next thing I knew she was behind me, standing on her hind feet as she gently, and quite deliberately I might add, nudged me into the shit- filled wheelbarrow with her knees. I fell in head first, shit faced with my cowboy hat bent out of shape, scrambling to get back up while she pranced circles around me, victoriously, celebrating her achievement.

Not nice! But lots of entertainment for all who saw this bit of comedic act at my expense. Nothing was hurt except for my ego and my hat!

Lucky!!

The shenanigans and vital lessons for a novice continued for several months until Christa was able to resume her job as the barn manager.

I made it out alive and back to my regular job. I had no particular interest in finding myself back in the same position again.

Viewpoints

It was only a couple years later that I found myself mucking full time at our new location in Aldergrove.

Mucking a few paddocks here or there is something that can be fun and enjoyable but not for over thirty horses. The latter can feel like hell on earth especially with harsh weather to contend with. Day after day, horse after horse. One can easily go insane after a while.

There are a few techniques I developed in order to become able to endure this never-ending nightmare that felt like the curse of Sisyphus at times.

The most important lesson I learned was the significance of the direction of my vision.

Literally!

In the multiple rows of paddocks filled with crap that needed cleaning, I learned quickly that if I looked up towards the paddocks that I had already cleaned and enjoyed the view of the tidy paddocks while mucking instead of looking down toward the remaining paddocks that were filthy and yet to be cleaned, I would feel much better, motivated and energized in getting my chores done.

It was amusing how such a subtle thing as looking to the left, as opposed to the right could make or break my spirit that day, further bringing light to the influence the smallest physical movements and changes in posture can have on our psyches. (Makes me wonder what kind of psychological effect the cell phone obsession has on us, as it requires us to walk around with our heads down in a submissive stance and frame instead of looking up and out like we used to. But I digress.)

This way of thinking has come in quite valuable with my training projects. You can really work yourself up into a frenzy thinking how much further you have to go with a training project with a limited amount of time and a whole lot of high expectations from your clients to hand them a broke, bombproof horse in three months!

But if you look at how much your horse has learned and accomplished instead of how much further they need to go, it changes the tone of the job not only for you but more importantly for your horse. Every day we look back on our advances and lessons learned, how far we've come, not how much further we have to go. How good certain things are now compared to when we first started. Celebrate our successes in order to gain momentum and energy to carry us through the rest of the way.

It's all in which direction you look at it, literally.

Informed by Shit

I am often amused by how so many sayings take on a literal interpretation with horses in the picture.

For example, take the term "shit disturber."

You walk into the paddock in the morning and the shit is scattered all over the place. Ground into the ground and spread out.

Well, you're dealing with a shit disturber!

Clearly the forensics give a telling tale of a horse who was running circles with his head up high in his paddock, picking fights with his neighbours and being a total nuisance!

Obviously this would give me a window to that horse's state of mind and prepare me for what to expect when working with him that day.

It could make the difference between choosing to take him straight to the round pen as opposed to risk bringing a feisty, energetic horse with an unsettled state of mind into the barn.

In contrast, his neighbour appears to have "kept her shit together" in nice, neat undisturbed piles. Clearly this horse had spent a quiet evening of eating and moseying along peacefully minding her footfall, keeping her shit together.

There's a lot of information you can gather from examining the state of the shit in a paddock. You can tell if the hay was agreeing with them or not by the consistency.

The number of piles you find can give you many clues. Overfed? Underfed? Dehydrated?

An exaggerated lack of shit could even be a sign of possible colic when considered in conjunction with other symptoms. Or maybe the horse is eating it, as sometimes is the case, indicating a deficiency in minerals.

If all in one pile, it could be that you're dealing with a stallion or recently gelded horse. It could even be a sign of possible soreness of feet or some kind of lameness that might be prohibiting the horse from their normal amount of movement in the paddock.

Not to mention monitoring and inspecting for the presence of parasites and worms.

Paying attention to such details also played a great role in psyching myself up for going into a paddock to muck. I wasn't just mindlessly picking anymore, I was checking to see what the shit told me about a horse's physical and psychological state of mind, like reading a daily report on each one. It gave the job a much higher "purpose." Once again finding myself learning and experiencing the value and importance of bringing "purpose" to the job I ask my horses to do.

There is great importance in noticing any change from the norm.

No animal I'm aware of notices subtle changes better than horses. If a bucket is usually on left side of the barn door but now is on the right for some reason, horses will notice and react ever so slightly or not so slightly. I've tried to adopt this neurotic OCD condition from horses to help me notice the slightest changes from the norm in their environment, surroundings and routine.

Some people are really good at this. I remember stealing my mom's car at the age of 14 before I had my license. I was so careful to park it back exactly where she had it. Exact same spot in the carport, even cleaning the mud and snow the tires had dragged in on the ground. She knew within seconds of looking at the car. Something was different. She detected a tiny bit of salt in the grooves of the tires!!!!

I was in deep shit.

5 NEW CHALLENGES

Every time we moved to a new place with a new set up, new challenges and lessons presented themselves. The lessons learned to survive in the Richmond location where we stalled horses were helpful but not totally relevant to the new challenges I faced on the 20 acres in Aldergrove.

Where I could once get away with leading a horse at the shoulder, from a stall to a paddock and back, this just wasn't cutting the mustard at the new location anymore.

I had to up my game.

Moving Horses

We had fields where we housed three to four horses at a time and, once grazed down and on the verge of being destroyed, the fields needed to be rotated and the horses needed to be moved.

One option was to move each horse, one at a time.

This had some negative consequences. The first taken to the new field had to leave his small herd and be left alone there, running the fence line frantically, until you arrived with the second horse, and inevitably, the last horse to move would be worked up to quite a frenzy having been left behind with all her buddies gone to the new spot.

The strategies I'd learned to deal with separation anxiety with horses going from stalls to paddocks were helpful but not enough. This was a whole other ball game with different dynamics. The bond developed between horses that live in a herd setting is much stronger than the one between horses in neighbouring stalls. With the stalls, you had the option of leaving the quieter, older horses for last, where that option was not available when dealing with a band of young horses in a field, full of piss and vinegar.

Furthermore, the intensity of the migration was much higher and more exaggerated than the shorter distances covered in the Richmond setting, as these fields were not close and some time was required to cover the distance, and the horses grew exponentially more worked up with each step in the trek.

It was extremely time consuming and left a much bigger window of opportunity for disaster to take place.

The obvious solution was to lead more than one horse a time. Two or three depending on the number of horses in each field, so that no single horse would be left alone.

This meant these horses, who were almost always led on the left, now also needed to be led on the right, which really meant I had to learn how to lead the horses on both sides. Not only that, but I had to learn to keep the horses from bickering and fighting each other with me caught in the middle, keep them walking at the same pace despite their natural gait, and most importantly not to allow them to get ahead of me.

Leading at the shoulder on the left simply was not an option anymore.

Clearly there was a need to establish some rules and regulations the horses were expected to follow, in the same manner as we have rules and regulations for traffic. Stop signs, speed limits, traffic lights: without these there would be chaos and much carnage. Same thing with leading horses, especially multiple ones!

Going back to things becoming literal with horses, in order to "lead" a horse I must technically be ahead of the horse. I think of it as the photo finish in a race: even if a single whisker on the nose of that horse is past your shoulder line, you are no longer in a "leading" position, therefore, I am no longer "leading" my horse. I am "driving." Which is fine, as long as I am aware of the significant change and difference between the two.

Ultimately I should be able to switch from a leading position to a driving position as easily as I switch leading from the left to the right and maintain control of my horse during the course. In fact these kinds of shifts in positions and sides are often employed during a simple trek.

Here's an example.

I lead my horse to the gate with my horse approximately three to four feet behind me. I open the gate and turn towards the horse, switching hands and "drive" my horse through the gate and past me. I then turn as I close the gate and switch back to leading.

A combination of skills was needed to be put to work simultaneously, all of which were based on owning the space. Without the lessons learned from Fire and many other equine teachers about space ownership, this task would have been a complete shit show and hard to achieve in safe and orderly manner.

Inspired by watching horses move together, I chose the Pontiac logo as my geometrical shape for this job, putting me at the tip of the arrow and the horses to the left and right, to the back and to the sides. There were a number of things I needed to practice and master in leading one horse before I could be successful at leading multiple horses. I had to practice leading a single horse at about three or four feet back and a couple feet over. I envisioned us being on separate parallel tracks. There would be no collision or getting run over if the tracks never crossed. This meant I needed to make the space directly behind me unavailable to the horses, which would later become crucial in leading multiple horses, as it would keep them from interacting and practicing politics behind my back!

The other thing I needed to establish was maintaining control of the pace. My horse was to slow down and speed up according to my chosen pace, not the other way around. This feature has many benefits. It requires my horse to stay focused on me, therefore rendering outside distractions much less important and pressing. I am, at all times, in competition for my horse's focus and attention with the rest of the world, be it other horses, cars, bags, barking dogs, deer in the bushes, cows mounting each other, whatever. The more reason and purpose I give my horses to pay attention to me, the less likely they are to react to other distractions.

Next step was to practice on both sides. Get as good with the right as with the left. I've found it extremely helpful to do everything I do with my right hand with the left as well. Ever tried saddling a horse from the right? Do it. Mounting. Dismounting. And of course, leading, driving. All of it. (I owe this to our friend Daryl, who would always make me saddle the horses from the right whenever we hosted a colt starting clinic for him. I owe him, my wife and many other human teachers a lot more than that, but I digress.)

Once confident and practiced at doing all that, I was able to add more horses to the equation. One on the left, and one on the right. Soon I was able to bring more than two. I would usually cap it to a maximum of four on line. Two on each side. But this was only possible by arranging them in accordance to the herd dynamics and hierarchy in that particular group.

Keeping the pressure off the lead lines was crucial to this exercise. Keeping the slack in the line, so the line becomes simply a conduit for information and direction instead physical force, was essential. But not so much slack that the line became dead and could no longer carry signal or get tangled in the horse's feet. I had to learn to eliminate all bracing and physical pulling and pushing to make the task safe and doable. Later on, from horseback, this became very useful in bringing in the whole herd, up to 15 horses, on a much larger acreage without the horses on line obviously, as the conversation became more and more about spatial relation of my body to theirs without the use of lead lines.

The Pontiac formation was key in this up-scaled challenge when on foot, but the single file directly behind me worked best when on horseback. On the fifty acre chunk of land we acquired for a few years, the horses often needed to be brought in from the far end of the acreage to the holding corral, where we would worm them, groom them and get their feet trimmed. This was usually done by choosing a horse that we knew the rest of the herd would follow, and riding bareback with a halter. The terrain had a lot of steep climbs and descents, so it was imperative to keep the herd behind me to prevent a full stampede from occurring and losing control over my horse, as they regularly enjoyed barreling down up and down these canyon trails at full tilt.

Bringing in the herd in winter

Space ownership did a fantastic job of maintaining order and pace. The herd knew not to run past the lead and follow the pace. It made no difference if I was leading or riding. The rules applied just the same.

This one simple rule is one of the most important aspects of leading a horse trouble free and safe: Never get ahead of me.

Looking back, breaking that rule was almost always the main culprit behind every leading disaster. The life and death importance of this rule became painfully clear to me when I almost got one of my horses killed.

Taking a water break before heading up the hill

Leading the herd up the hill

Cisco

Back in the Aldergrove location, I had decided to lead one of my horses off property to further expose him to the outside world. The ranch was tucked away at the end of a cul-de-sac, and there wasn't that much traffic until you finally got to one of the main roads that merged to Hwy 13. I wanted to take Cisco, the troubled mustang, there to expose him to some heavy traffic coming and going, so if we wanted to ride out to one of the parks he wouldn't be frightened by the cars and trucks on that stretch. Cisco was doing fine with the occasional car coming and going so I decided to up the ante and take him right on the road with cars whizzing past us from front and back. There were a lot of cars as it was the beginning of rush hour. Cisco was doing remarkably well. So we turned around and started heading back, trying to leave things on a good note.

We started back with me on the left, buffering him from the traffic coming from behind, with the fence of a rescue farm on his right hand side.

That's when the unexpected happened.

A number of species of animals, including pigs, chickens, goats, ducks, miniature donkeys and few others decided to rush the fence from behind the bush to take a good look at my horse at the exact same time a car was coming up behind us. This frightened Cisco to no end and he spooked. He ran past me and as he hit the end of the lead line, he turned and came back, now facing me on my left hand side, on a head-on collision course with the car coming up behind me.

Of course as usual all this happened in a split second. There was nothing to do except wait for the impact and deal with the dreaded aftermath. It was only by sheer luck that the car coming up from behind had a responsible, savvy driver who saw the whole thing unfolding and stopped the vehicle about 10 feet behind me, leaving me ample room to get a hold of my horse and move off to safety.

Cisco could have easily died that day.

But we survived to learn an incredibly important lesson: my horses must learn not to ever run past me without my asking, no matter what.

This became a huge part of my training and something I would practice until it became second nature to the horse.

Being a Leader

I was working a nervous mare and we were heading to the round pen between a fence and a manure bin that had a tarp on it. She had nowhere to go except forwards or back. As we passed the bin the wind picked up the tarp, flapping it around, making some scary noises, the ones that trigger flight. I could hear the frantic scramble of feet behind me, but all I had to do without even looking back was lift the palm of my right hand with a subtle twist of my wrist upwards. The mare, well-practiced at the rules of leading behind me, came to a beautiful sliding stop to avoid passing me, and it paid off for her. I got her out of the tight squeeze safe and sound. I find the amount of trust and confidence we can build in our horses with such a simple practice is far greater and more rewarding than "bombproofing" our horses.

There is so much opportunity that we can build on to establish a solid relationship during the simple task of leading a horse as long as it is done with certain rules, regulations and methodology in place.

Another very important ingredient is the proper body language and posture needed when we have been trusted by our horse with the task of leading. That's where it all begins. Without this none of the other parts can be achieved.

Of course, as usual, things get literal again.

We talked about how in order to lead you literally have to be in a leading position. However, there's another literal aspect to it. In order to "lead" effectively you must also embody the essence of a "leader." Your posture must replicate that of a leader. Your body language must be indicative of a fearless and brave captain, to boldly go where no one and no horse have gone before. I like using Captain Kirk as the perfect model for an ideal leader. He would always respect and consult his crew for advice without losing his position or creating doubt in his abilities as the one in charge. He would always go the distance to protect his crew, and he would never let his personal relationships with the crew interfere with his decision making which always prioritized the wellbeing of those he was responsible for. He had the air of a leader, the posture and mannerisms. And he never took advantage or abused his sacred position.

Here are a few things I have noticed about how a leader acts that I try to incorporate into leading horses.

A leader looks ahead and out and does not stare at the followers. It is the job of those who follow to keep an eye on the leader, not the other way around. The leader's job is to scan the surroundings and look to where she's going. It's easy to confuse your horse as to who is supposed to be doing what if you're constantly staring at them while "leading." It makes them question who is in charge of navigating the course.

Good leaders are followed willingly, not through force. I don't have to physically enforce my asks if the horse has accepted me as worthy for the lead position. They will, pardon the pun again, just follow my lead and trust me. This is how I am able to use my lead line primarily as a means of communication instead of physical enforcement or restraint. The lead line becomes a two-way line of communication between my horse and me that allows me to know where my horse is and what he's up to without me having to constantly look back to check. The line, in turn, sends signals and messages from me to the horse to remind and guide him of where he should be and what he should be doing. But none of that is possible until I have learned to act as a leader.

I don't see a point in putting a halter on a horse, restraining them, limiting their mobility and compromising their safety unless we have learned to become true, trustworthy and capable leaders. Not everyone is comfortable or suited for this kind of position that comes with a tremendous amount responsibility and know-how. It takes a certain kind of person with certain characteristics. Maybe that's why not everyone is qualified to be part of the cavalry. Becoming a horseman is serious business and should be taken as such. Horses are capable of establishing all kinds of relationships with people, many of which don't necessarily require the person to be the leader, but those relationships can be limiting in what activities a person and a horse can do together, as I learned with Cisco, almost at the cost of his life. Anyone can become a leader if they want to. It just takes a lot of work, courage, respect for and understanding of the position and a willingness to change, to make mistakes, to get hurt. No one is born knowing how to do this stuff. We must take the time, choose the right venue and ask for help from professionals and trainers to get us there. We owe it to our horses to do the work needed to get the job done.

There is no end to learning the art of leading a horse properly, it contains almost everything we need to establish a balanced functional relationship with our horses.

A False Sense of Confidence

Earlier I touched on a couple of things. One, everything a horse gives you is a gift even if you think you've earned it. Two, things can get dangerous if you take them for granted and get too comfortable.

I remember my first training project, Naari, a three-year-old Arab gelding. Total punk and a bitch to handle. He liked nipping and had gone as far as pawing handlers, including me, while being led. He was temperamental and a spoiled brat. Fire's son. I decided I was going to try to get something going with this guy, see how far I could get with tacking and backing, with neither one of us having ever done anything like that before. I picked a quiet time of the summer when most people were away, so I could fail in peace and privacy. Just me and the horse with no one to "tsk" at me.

Not knowing what the hell to do, I decided to just go and spend time with him in his field. Just sit there and wait for him to come around to see what I was doing. Which he would. With no halter or specific agenda we spent time like this together for about week, practicing the things his father had taught me with moving around each other and relating. On the eighth day I haltered him and brought him out. He led much better and didn't horse around like he used to.

Gradually we moved our sessions to the round pen where we played around with some tarps and saddle pads, things I'd seen trainers do. Not much longer after that, I brought out the saddle. He didn't seem concerned at all. We had trust and he was game, intrigued and up for new things. I clumsily got the saddle on and off without cinching it a bunch of times. Left it at that, came back to it the next day when I decided to finally cinch it up. He stood still, not concerned. Once in a while checking out what I was doing and then losing interest again. The saddle was cinched and I sent him out. He walked around with no objections, so I asked for a trot and then a canter. He couldn't care less. Never bucked or even remotely got bothered. So I looped my lead rope around and made some reins for my halter and just got on.

Nothing.

A little leg pressure and he moved out. Carrying me quietly and confidently.

Holy shit!!!

I did it.

This is easy!!! I just started a horse and I hardly know how to ride!! HA!!!

Naari had made it easy. Way too easy.

As did the next four horses I "started."

I was clumsy and didn't have any rhyme or reason with anything I did. I got away with murder and I became extremely complacent about the whole process. I remember thinking, either I'm a genius and an incredibly gifted horseman or everybody else is a total idiot. "This shit is easy!!! What's the big deal?" I thought to myself.

I was ready to learn my next lesson.

I had just pulled off a miracle with a two-year-old Lipizzaner who had spooked, gotten away from his handler with the rope dangling behind him, ran himself into some barbed wire, cut his nut sack open and gelded himself. From that point on he would not be haltered and was terrified of ropes. The owner, a client of my wife, was close to putting him down when I convinced her to let me work with him. She was hesitant as I wasn't experienced, but agreed.

Using similar methods to those I had employed with Naari by just hanging out in his field, I managed to pique his interest and gain enough trust that I was able halter him. But he was still terrified of the lead line and ropes and would bolt, tearing the rope out of my hands. Then I got lucky again. In one of his attempts to pull the rope out of my hands and run, I, quite by accident, managed to position myself at the perfect angle with his head slightly to the inside which resulted in him pulling his own legs out from underneath him when he tried to take off. He was in disbelief. After that he quit trying to pull the rope out of my hands as he thought I somehow had the power to take him down. From there I was able to work with him with various ropes and objects, building up his confidence to the point where his rope phobias disappeared and he became quite functional.

Our client was beyond impressed and I was on cloud nine, thinking, "Man I'm really something special. Holy shit!"

She asked me if I would start her 12-year-old Lipizzaner brood mare. Just to the point where she could be tacked and backed. Nothing more than that.

Piece of cake. Of course I can! I'm a freakin' genius!

I almost feel like I don't need to tell you what happened next, but I will.

We started out with some basic ground work. This mare was confident and not easy to spook, which was great. What wasn't great was this defiant, annoyed bitch face she greeted me with every time we spent time together. She didn't think I was charming or amusing at all. She gave me the impression that she thought of me as a bit of an idiot, a bit of a clown. She was not amused in the least bit and was serious and unimpressed. Not just with me, but in general. In fact, upon, dropping off the mare, the owner said, "Say hello to Anja, a.k.a 'The Bitch.'"

That should have been my first clue.

The second clue that I didn't take to heart was when I took Anja for a walk around the property. She was leading confidently behind me when I heard a thud, a yelp and another thud, with some rustling sounds in the bush.

I looked behind me to find our blue heeler, Daisy, lying in the bush yelping and crying. "What the hell?" I wondered. Daisy's ball lay close to the Lippi mare's hind feet. "Oh no."

It seems that Daisy had run up to Anja from behind with her ball and in response Anja had kicked her hard, sending her flying ten feet, snapping her femur in two. She had done all this without spooking or skipping a single beat while we walked. Just wham!! Any other horse would have spooked, jumped forward and then maybe kicked out. Not her.

[In case you're wondering, Daisy survived and now has a metal pin in her leg.]

Hmmm.

We moved to the next phase of me not knowing what the hell I was doing, with me sacking her out in the arena. I was all over her with my hands and ropes and nothing seemed to worry her. She was bothered but only because I was annoying her, not because I was scaring her.

I tried sidling her up to a little step mounting block and started putting some pressure and weight on her back. But I couldn't quite slide up on her back. I wanted to, but she was really round and I couldn't get her as close as I wanted to the mounting block; that was my third missed clue.

I fumbled around with that like an idiot for a while, trying to get her closer to the mounting block with no success. So I decided to try leaping up on her back from where I was. I looped the rope and made reins and got ready to hop on. I grabbed a chunk of mane and went for it. I made it! I was up there. Bareback. She was pissed.

She scooted forward at a fast trot for thirty feet or so and slammed on the brakes. I managed to stay on. Not a pretty sight, but I stayed on. Holy Shit! I did it again! I just rode her. She's broke!!! I'm a genius!!!

Proud of myself, I slid off and put her away. "We'll pick it up from here tomorrow," I said, triumphantly.

The next day I set it up the same. Only she would not come anywhere near the mounting block. Every time I'd even think about hopping on, she'd put herself just far enough from the block so that I couldn't.

"What the hell, mare? You're broke . . . ish. I already rode you! Fine! We will work on getting a saddle on you and then I'll be able to get on with no issues," I figured, frustrated.

So we started the saddle work and things went pretty smooth. She never bucked or showed any signs of being bothered through the tacking process. She moved out with the cinch tight and was just fine - annoyed, but fine.

"Great! I'm great! She's great! This is great!" I thought.

"Now, let's pick it up where we left it off a few days ago. Back to riding."

Still in a halter, I reached over with my right hand and gripped the outside skirting of the saddle. With my left hand I held the makeshift reins and a chunk of mane. I put my left foot in the stirrup and proceeded to pull myself up and into the saddle.

I never made it.

About halfway there, the mare took off bucking with me dangling off the side. I couldn't break free. My fingers were stuck under the saddle skirting. It seemed like an eternity, but she finally stopped as she took herself straight into the fence like she'd done the first time. I was finally able to make sense of what had happened. Through all the crow-hopping and bucking, the saddle had swung down so the horn was now pointing at my belly. My left foot was still in the stirrup and had swung underneath her belly and my index and middle fingers on the right hand were pinned under the skirting of the saddle. I was only a few strides away from certain death. Had she gone any further, I would have ended up completely underneath her with my foot still stuck in the stirrup, and quite possibly dead.

So . . . that was the fifth horse I "started."

It became crystal clear to me that I had no idea what the hell I was doing.

It became blatantly clear to me that the previous four had humoured and accommodated me well over and beyond my skills and capabilities.

It became clear to me that I needed help and had a shit load to learn about horses, riding and colt starting.

And with that a never ending string of failures and accidents began.

But I didn't give up.

Fire had given me a taste of how things could be and should be. I wanted it back. I wanted to learn how to create that and feel that again.

Anja and I ended up working things out eventually to achieve the end goal her owner had in mind, a picture of her with a saddle on and me in it.

Rethinking Myself as Trainer

Horses seem to have perfect timing and know when to teach you the right lesson at the right time. In trying to improve my riding and gain more experience in the saddle, I decided it would be wise to spend some time with our school horses. This, I thought, would give me a better fighting chance, to learn on a horse that is used to having novices on his back. Oliver was the perfect horse for the job. A trusty, mature Arabian that had been with my wife since she was a youngster, a perfect gentleman and master with young novice riders, the ultimate savvy and wise teacher in our lessons program.

"I can ride him. I've ridden green horses for crying out loud. Surely I have nothing to worry about with Oli."

So I tacked him up and hit the trails.

A little later, I came back to the barn, ghost white, and complained to Christa, "What the hell is wrong with this horse? He tried to buck me off and then tried to break my nose by whipping his head back at me! Three times!!!"

Christa didn't believe me. He had NEVER EVER in all his years done anything like that to anyone who had ever ridden him. Well he did to me!

I had to show her to prove it and he didn't disappoint. Christa watched in sheer amazement and amusement as Oli tried to knock my head off and bucked and hopped around the arena, re-enacting the whole mess in the trails.

He did not care for my cocky attitude. He did not care for my lack of respect for the job, he did not care for me taking him for granted, and he didn't care for me taking liberties with him.

I got the message loud and clear and realized I needed some serious doses of reality and manners.

It seems with each lesson learned the horses raised their expectations and upped the ante on me. Each horse would find a new way to humble me, demanding that I get better.

A False Sense of Entitlement

Vega is my boy. Well he's Ginger and Fire's boy really, but I always think of him as my boy. He's a ¾ Arabian, 1/4 Appaloosa. He was born in our field and has known me since the moment he came out. He is family. Vega was always casual, aloof and never showed any signs of fear or insecurity. Not that I was aware of it at the time, but this made things difficult for us. I never got an opportunity to offer him any kind of help, as he never felt like he actually needed any. He was an easy start and seemed to be ready for anything.

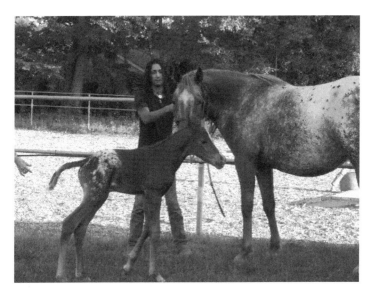

Vega with mom Ginger

Vega didn't need a lot from me and I began to take that for granted. He never complained and went along with whatever. That made it possible for me to skip a lot of steps and treat him like a schooled grown-up without much time or work put into his education. I used to ride

Baby Vega

him out bareback with a rope halter, park under a tree, take a nap on his back when the weather was nice, do chores, work horses, push cows around. Saddled or bareback, it didn't matter. Load him in a trailer and go wherever and do whatever, not worried about the fact that hey, we've never done that before. "He'll be fine, he's *my* boy." That was always my answer.

I was a little bit strict and had some high expectations of him. It wasn't uncommon for me to get frustrated if he didn't get things right, right away. This was practically the opposite of how I was with my paying training jobs. I was much more patient, consistent, diligent, forgiving and thorough with other people's horses.

I felt like if Vega didn't succeed at doing something, it reflected badly on *me* and *my* skills, despite the fact that I never really put in the time with him, placing unfair expectations on my unprepared horse.

This was not a balanced relationship, and Vega worked hard to compensate for my shortcomings in the partnership. He gave a lot, and I took and asked for more, because he's my boy!

Our business was growing in Aldergrove and in an effort to create more space for paying spots at the ranch, we decided to send off a few of our horses to live on an acreage just outside of Osoyoos. Since I was so busy and didn't have a lot of time for Vega, he got to be one of the ones to go for a vacation.

On the trail

We'd visit the horses regularly, until winter came and driving the Crowsnest Highway was just not worth the risk. A couple of months went by before we were able to go visit again, spend some time with the horses and trim their feet. We located the horses and I haltered Vega to pick his feet. Well, it was a bit of a horror show. Though showing no signs of lameness, Vega had gotten a pretty severe cut on his front right hoof. It looked like he may have gotten it caught in some wire and had just about pulled off the whole foot in an effort to free himself. We always take the time to teach our horses not to pull when their feet get caught. Usually they stand still and wait for someone to come and cut them loose, which would happen pretty quickly at home, with so many boarders and so much traffic going in and out of each field. But not out here. We don't know for how long Vega waited before he realized no one was coming and he had to get out of the mess by himself or die. Round bales were put out for the horses once every two weeks, so he could have gone a long time without anyone knowing he needed help.

The wound looked a few weeks old and was healing, so there was no point in calling the vet. He was not lame and was getting around okay, so we left it at that. The physical scars were going to be there for life, but what about the psychological ones?

Vega had developed a little bit of a phobia with anything gripping at his ankles and had lost some dexterity and would trip a lot under saddle, possibly due to some nerve damage on that foot. I brought him back home that summer. I decided to spend a little more time with him and work on all that. We revisited some simple exercises of leading him by the foot with the rope. A bit apprehensive, but he did well. So I decided to move on to something a little more challenging, something we hadn't tried before.

I looked around and saw this sack on a length of rope we had. "I'll get on and we'll drag this thing around. Sounds good. It's easy and safe. If anything happens just let go of the rope and we're free."

We dragged the sack around the perimeter of the pen and he was fine. We then dragged it to the centre of the covered round pen. I let the rope out so we could ride away from it for about twenty feet or so and had him stand with the sack positioned at the centre of his barrel, on his right side. From that position, I started to reel the sack in towards us. Nice and slow. Paying close attention to his comfort level, I reeled the sack closer and closer. He looked at it a couple of times and didn't seem concerned. I pulled the sack up to about ten feet from where we stood and stopped. We just sat there for a bit processing. He was still chill. I wondered if I could reel it up, all the way up, so I could grab it and we could carry it around. With this in mind, I tugged on the rope with a bit of force as it seemed to have gotten stuck behind a ripple of sand in the arena. The bag jumped a little to clear the sandy obstacle. That got Vega's attention, making him do a quick turn towards the sack, putting it directly in front of him and positioning the rope rubbing against his right side, all the way from the ground by his right foot up to my hand which was still gripping the end of the rope.

I had promised myself to just let go of the rope if anything happened. But there was no time. As Vega made the first turn towards the sack, not only did the rope end up on his right hand side with the sack towards him, but he pulled the damn thing closer yet, so it looked like the sack was coming right at him!

Vega spun again, completing his initial 90° turn to a full 180°, which meant the rope was now wrapped around from his right, coming across the front legs to the left. So what he then saw with his left eye was the sack coming at him from the left, which made him spin away, completing the 180° turn into to a full 360°, wrapping us up in the rope all the way around all four feet.

Things became a bit of blur from that point. I felt like I was in the washing machine during the spin cycle. He kept spinning and running and spinning and getting more and more tangled up.

All I remember was thinking, "This could be it. Today could be the day I die horsing around. Just stay up there. Stay calm. Stay with your horse. Don't pull on his face. Give him his head. There's nothing you can do but sit centered and wait." The slightest imbalance to the left or right and I would have been on the ground, under his spinning and spastic feet. Lessons learned from fear management had kicked in so I was able to think myself through a life threatening situation.

It seemed like an eternity, but he finally stopped, huffing, trying to catch his breath. I had a split second window of opportunity to do something, to save my life and his. I scanned the situation real quick and saw that the rope was wrapped around the horn. I quickly unwrapped it. The end of the rope fell to the ground and he miraculously managed to step out of the whole mess, free of the blasted thing.

I don't know how we made it out. But we did. And we got to live another day.

I decided maybe we'd take a break from ropes for a while and go do other things.

Fun things.

Safe things.

However, the once very confident and aloof Vega was now showing some signs of insecurity and distrust in everything we did. He, for good reason, was no longer believing me that I could keep him safe and make good decisions.

I knew this, and the harder I tried to "work on the problem," the worse things got.

I had always had high expectations of Vega even though I had not put a lot of time and effort into our relationship. Having finally run out of his gifted and my unearned trust, I was hell-bent on making up for lost time.

But that's not how it works.

The harder I tried, the more I stressed him out.

My level of expectations out of the sessions got higher and higher, and the intensity drove him further and farther away from me, as the gravitational pull between us grew weak.

A reversal of polarity had begun to take place.

It was blatantly obvious. He would do what I asked of him in the round pen, but his mind was elsewhere. Like a student looking out the window during class, he just wasn't interested. Everything I asked for he gave, but in a robotic, mechanical manner with no real feel or passion behind it, without really looking at me, just going through the motions.

I had managed to shut my horse down.

One day, busy with all the work I had to do, I found myself with a small window of free time and decided to take Vega out for a quick ride in the trails, down to the creek and back, something we had done many times before over the years. Vega was distracted and not happy about leaving his buddy behind in his field. As we headed out toward the trails we could still hear his field buddy calling out to him. Vega felt resistant, abrasive and argumentative. He was zig-zagging and refusing to move straight. We grew more and more frustrated with each other until I finally decided to lay the law down and give him a swift kick in the ribs to stop him from bracing and pushing against my leg. That's all the excuse he need to get rid of me. In a split second he did a 180 into the leg that had kicked him, and took off running and bucking. I was catching a lot of air between me and the saddle with each buck. My only saving grace was that he maintained a straight line. Had he swerved the slightest, I would have ended up on my ass or head. After about fifty yards of this, he came to a halt and I got him "under control." It felt ugly. He was huffing and puffing, complying with my exaggerated commands - not asks, commands - over his quarters as I disengaged the hind and moved the shoulders with anger. The anger that stemmed from him scaring the crap out of me. He was listening and complying, but I knew very well that I did not have a horse. I didn't have a partner and the relationship had suffered greatly.

I wasn't ready to let go.

I couldn't.

The thought of our relationship having soured didn't sit well with me, and I became even more determined to save the partnership.

I needed to win his trust again, and the best way I knew how was to go through some basic confidence building exercises. So, like an idiot, I decided to go back to working with him in the round pen with the sack on the rope. "If I can get him through this phobia I will win his respect and admiration again, and we can go back to having the kind of relationship we used to have," I thought, foolishly.

But this time I would be smart. I would work with him from the ground with the sack on the rope, so I could really help him and support him through the process should the shit hit the fan again.

Vega was saddled and I had him in a rope halter with the sack on the line towing behind him. He was very apprehensive, but I was sure I could manage the situation no matter what.

The rope towing the sack came up from behind and over the saddle, behind the horn and around. It was not dallied; it just half looped behind and came around the inside of the horn. This way I could keep the sack directly behind him as he dragged it. Feeling unsure and insecure, Vega kicked out as the rope brushed up against his left hind leg. This would have normally been fine, except it wasn't a regular straight kick, he kind of kicked out sideways, in a swooping motion, and managed to hook the rope around his fetlock in a split second.

This freaked him right out and he kicked at it a couple more times, each time resulting in more wraps and drawing the sack closer to his leg. That's when he completely lost it and switched to "running blind" mode, barreling right through me, knocking me out of the way with his head down, honking, ripping the lead line right out of my hands. Now there were two ropes attacking him. The sack rope and the lead line.

Vega was doing laps in the round pen, wrapped tight in both ropes with a sack attached snug to his left foot.

This was by far the worst scenario I could have ever created. He did lap after lap after lap, kicking out, harder and harder. So hard that he managed to put a couple of holes right through the wall panels of the pen made of made of ¾ inch plywood set in steel pipe frames. I had never see anything like it.

I stood there in complete horror, trying to keep my cool, and my head in thinking mode. He was now completely wrapped in both ropes. I kept trying to get a good look and spot where would be the best place to cut the rope if I ever get the chance. He stopped. And stood still, dripping in sweat.

This could be good.

He may have worked his way through this fear.

He may have just had a major breakthrough.

I took my knife out and walked up cautiously, eyeing the spot I wanted to cut, while saying in a shaky voice "Easy boy. Easy..."

I decided to go for the thickest cluster of wraps around the horn to make the cut. He was standing still and it seemed like he was done running. So I quickly began cutting into the rope around the horn.

The second I cut through he started again, coming right at me, knocking me back, but I stayed on my feet. For that I was grateful, as I was able to side step, in a hurry, out of his way. He was off again like the Tasmanian devil.

But I had something worse to worry about now.

The knife was no longer in my hand!

The knife was missing!

Where's the fuckin' knife???

I checked my body to see if it was in me. It wasn't. Was it in him???

Oh shit!!!

I couldn't tell. He was still running like mad, but having cut the ropes he finally became untangled, free from the sack attack and stopped a second time. This time for good.

I walked up to him and grabbed what was left of the lead line and started examining him to see if the knife was lodged in him.

There was no blood.

He did seem lame on the left hind as he wasn't putting any weight on it. He'd been kicking pretty hard with that leg for quite a while. I checked his body all over and to my relief couldn't find the knife. Just looking at his left hind would now set him to kick again.

We did eventually find the knife buried in a heap of sand under one of the panels in the round pen. But that wasn't of much consolation to me.

I had ruined my horse.

It was over.

I wasn't sure how much damage had been done to his trust and confidence in me. I assumed, at that point, that he'd never let me touch his hind left again. I brought him into the barn the next day and asked him to pick it up for me. He gave it and let me pick it out. What a relief. Either he had forgiven me, or he hadn't associated my hand's touch to the sack.

It was time for some serious reflection as to what went wrong and how we could try to salvage the relationship.

I needed to shut up and listen.

A few days later we went back to the round pen. Vega was still somewhere else in his mind. There was no point in doing anything. So I just put him away.

He needed a break from me. He needed a break from "training." He needed a break from me trying to fix things, as I was clearly achieving the opposite.

I had been here before.

I realized I had become way too "*wrapped*" up in being a trainer again. I had lost sight of the lessons Fire had taught me in the early days.

I had lost sight of the basic principles and the simplicity of two bodies sharing space with no agendas or ulterior motives.

Delusions of Grandeur had me looking at horses as notches in my trainer's belt. I needed to step back and get back to my shit-picking roots and philosophy.

I decided to take all the "training" out of my interactions with Vega, and just spend time with him, without asking for anything. If he wanted to come over and get some scratches that was fine. If he didn't, that was fine too. It didn't matter. I was just happy to see him and share some space with him at whatever distance and proximity he chose and was comfortable with. I'd only halter him and hold him to get his feet trimmed by Christa, which would only happen once every six weeks, and that's it. During his haltering, he would very subtly express his existing mistrust of ropes. I acknowledged his concerns and listened, but did not try to fix it, just kept it at a comfortable level for him.

This went on for quite a while until I noticed Vega getting increasingly more interested in not just hanging out, but coming with and doing something, maybe go somewhere, see some things.

One sunny summer day, over a year after all the mishaps had occurred, I brought Vega into the round pen to check things out. He was all eyes and ears on me, happy and excited to get back to doing things.

What a gift, what luck!

But as usual being busy trying to earn a living, our interactions remained far and few in between. "But that's okay, he's with the herd and has a life," and I figured as long as the few interactions we did have were positive ones, then we were making some kind of progress.

I needed to undo the fear of failure I had instilled in him. I needed to take the pressure off and listen to his concerns, offer him support, without him worrying about disappointing me. I needed to treat him like I do other people's horses, not as MY boy. More forgiving, less strict, with reasonable expectations and getting back to having fun. Free him of my possessive chains of expectations and respect him as an individual, not as something that belongs to me. If anyone's got a claim on him, it's his mother, Ginger, not me.

Siesta time with Vega

Vega assisting me with teaching this young mustang to pony politely over a few sessions

Camping with Vega

6 WHAT'S IN IT FOR THE HORSE?

Moving horses out to a piece of land in Pritchard to make space for paying clients in Aldergrove was one of the most eye opening events for me that has occurred during my entire shit picking career to date.

Before we finally moved the business to our current quarter section location in Pritchard and were still operating out of Aldergrove, we had purchased fifty acres of land just across the Thompson River from where would eventually end up. It was dirt cheap and had nothing on it. So we had the perimeter fenced and rolled the dice on hitting water in an area that is notorious for being dry with hard-to-find, low-producing aquifers that give poor quality water.

We lucked out. We hit water and plenty of it! Twenty gallons per minute of pristine water that did not need treating.

We built a couple of shelters, put in a heated automatic waterer and a pump house, and parked an old RV there. We worked it out with one of our neighbours, who had also built the fence, to put out a couple round bales for us once a week as we had no farm equipment, barn or anything else there.

We weren't sure how things were going to go. Time would tell. As it turned out things worked out really well for the horses who stayed there. A little too well. Soon there was a long waiting list of people from the lower mainland who wanted their horses sent up there as well. The benefits were very attractive. The climate was much dryer, and therefore way more suitable for the horses. Their feet improved from the constant movement on varied terrain; they put on muscle and lost soft fat; their spirits picked up with minimal care and interference from us. We'd go up once or twice a month to check on them, groom them, trim their feet when needed, worm them, and that's all.

Meanwhile back in Aldergrove I was slaving away, twelve hour days, seven days a week, caring and maintaining, picking shit!

It had been even worse at the Richmond location, where we first started, despite the fact that we'd had less than half the number of horses we were looking after in Aldergrove. There were stalls in addition to paddocks and we were feeding flakes as well as maintaining individual water buckets for each horse. It was all very time consuming and labour intensive.

As an added "bonus" the horses were more agitated and much less healthy!

Yay!!

The whole idea of moving to Aldergrove in the first place was to give the horses more space and opportunity to live in small herds. It only made sense. They're social animals and we wanted to try to set them up with a living arrangement that was closer to their natural way of life. Even in the paddocks, the horses were always in each other's company and able to interact and touch over the fence. It improved things drastically in contrast to the set up in Richmond. And things improved a hundred times more in Pritchard in contrast to the set up in Aldergrove.

There was an important correlation to be noted.

The closer we got to the "correct" and healthy living arrangement for the horses, the less laborious and time consuming my job got. As we all know, horses are not meant to live in confinement, segregated from one another. They're not designed for that. So, obviously, the farther we get from the way they were meant to live, the more obstacles we encounter and the harder we have to work to maintain our disgruntled horses.

So what the hell had I been doing all this time? Working myself to the bone picking up after these guys? For what?

You can always tell you're on the right path with horses when things get easier and more effortless. Same in the saddle, same on the ground, same with caring and doing chores. Everything just falls in to place for you and the horses when you're on the right track.

There was something else in the balance that was changing as well, something I touched on earlier in the book. The less laborious the job got, the higher the level of horsemanship was required to compensate.

The amount of horsemanship I needed to get the job done in Richmond was minimal compared to the skills I had to acquire in Aldergrove, which were minimal in contrast to the level of horsemanship I needed in order to function on wide open space in Pritchard.

The less we interfered with the horses, the better they did.

This was a dangerous line of thought in that it had a clear, logical conclusion to it. If we really cared for horses we needed to set them free and stop fencing them in. They're better off without us! We should stop messing with them altogether.

It's clear to me how they have improved my life, but what have I done for them?

What do I have to offer the horses in compensation for what they bring me?

The sad reality of the situation for all species is that our species has taken over the world. There are not many places left where animals can run free without eventually running into a fence!

We are on top of the food chain and we run the planet, badly I might add, but still, we run it.

There's an obvious advantage for horses, being masters at survival, to buddy up with the most dangerous and dominant species on the planet, Homo sapiens.

Imagine if you were dropped off in the jungle with no means of protection, who would you want to have as your buddy?

I always say the Lion.

If I befriended the Lion, the top of the food chain, King of the Jungle, I'd feel pretty safe.

Perhaps that's us to horses.

When they live in our world, we can offer them protection. We can make sure they have food, water and medical care when needed and help them navigate this fenced world and become functional in a partnership with us. A partnership that could give them back a new version of freedom. One that has us sitting on their backs.

I believe there can be a healthy, mutually beneficial partnership between us and horses, but we have to meet them at least halfway. Educate ourselves to their physical and psychological needs and satisfy them. Put in the time and work to improve our horsemanship, treat them with respect as individuals, not props for our pleasure, glory or as fancy pets. **The identity and purpose horses give us shouldn't have to cost them theirs.**

I've had a policy with my kids that they were not allowed to keep pets that had to be caged or locked up. If they weren't running free and sharing our space I didn't want them in the house. That was hard to reconcile with looking out the window and seeing horses standing in paddocks.

There's an awesome thing we learned when we moved out to the country. Fences here are not built to keep animals in. They're built to keep them out!

Up here they roam around and do whatever they want. Things feel different, the neighbours' animals are all over the dirt road, up the hill, in the valley, wherever they want to go. You only put fences up where you don't want them to go.

Our herd at Pritchard

You fence in your home and belongings you don't want them messing with.

It's the opposite.

Up here, you fence them out, not in!

It makes a profound difference.

I realize this is not a feasible setting for everyone to access, but what we can at least do is to acknowledge and understand what the horse is experiencing under average living conditions in barns and farms. There are always things we can do to try to compensate and improve the conditions. Take them out more often; horses need to move all the time. Feed them according to the way their digestive system functions. Let them socialize. Try different activities, disciplines, to make life more interesting for them. Trailer them out to parks and different places. Let them be horses.

But there's something else that we can bring to the picture that horses might find attractive aside from us providing for them. It's that something I felt and experienced initially between Fire and me. The day he showed me the way and helped me experience the power, joy and magic that can exist when our species move together in harmony and as one. With proper horsemanship we can empower our horses as they do us. In a healthy setting and through relationship we can elevate and benefit each other in ways that we cannot on our own. Only then can we justify taking everything they're giving us, knowing we're giving something back.

Fire greeting the barn cat

Manufactured by Amazon.ca
Bolton, ON

13077638R00085